MY GREAT BIG POSITIVE LIFE

FOR PARENTS

LORNA PARK

CONTENTS

PART THREE
MIND, BODY AND SOUL

FOREWORD

I recently read an article which highlighted the fact that as parents we are pretty good at discussing with our kids the changes they will face in their bodies as they grow, but that it's not so often that we will sit them down and discuss the changes that will happen within their brain.

During puberty the brain changes and grows more than at any other time (apart from when they are babies) and it is during this time that patterns (positive or negative) are wired into the brain hard and fast.

Our mental wellbeing effects everything in our lives, from our ability to be successful, our relationships with others to our physical health. It distresses me to constantly be reading that our kids are growing up more stressed out and anxious than ever before, with little resilience and unable to cope with the challenges of life.

Life has got so busy, so noisy, and so full of things that we are losing ourselves in our possessions. Constantly craving more and more we are so caught up in this fast moving, ever changing world, that we are losing sight of what makes us truly happy.

For the past few decades the measurement of happiness seems to have focused on how successful we are, how much money we have and what our life looks like with the importance of happiness, creativity, empathy, kindness, self awareness and emotional wellbeing seemingly gotten lost somewhere along the way.

We as adults are struggling to cope so it's no wonder our children are following suit.

And lets not forget that our children are having to navigate a whole new world driven by tech and the added pressure of growing up within a culture of comparison dominated by the rise of social media.

The good news is that society as a whole is now recognising the importance of taking care of ourselves mentally in the same way that a couple of decades ago we recognised and accepted that exercise and eating healthily was good for our physical health. Alongside this fascinating new research within the world of Neuroscience and the development of the Science of Positive Psychology in particular has changed the landscape in terms of previous held beliefs.

Practices that 20 years ago would have been seen as a bit

woo woo are now becoming mainstream, all backed up with scientific evidence that they work.

And they do work, I can personally vouch for that.

As someone who has suffered from anxiety I know first hand what living with a mental health issue can be like. It can come out of nowhere, apparently for no reason and it can be paralysing.

It's hard to look back and think about all the opportunities that I gave up on because of ..."what if?" "who do you think you are?" or " you're not good enough"

I wish I had understood what it was earlier, I wish I had realised that there was things I could have done to make it better sooner.

Most of all I wish it hadn't taken me to watch my son change from being a happy outgoing confident boy to one that was anxious, scared and stressed out, for me to realise that I needed to do something to address my own issues and his.

At this time I was lucky enough to be introduced to the work of award winning Positive Psychologist and Author Niyc Pidgeon and she opened my eyes to the world of Positive Psychology (the science of happiness), Growth Mindset and Mindfulness.

I became fascinated with the concept of really thriving and

not just surviving; what she described as self healing. This included concentrating on things like meditation, yoga, gratitudes, affirmations, intentions, kindness, connection and creating positive daily habits.

Once I started to put into practice the principles held at the centre of the science of happiness everything changed.

For my son I couldn't believe how quickly this happened for him. His young and curious mind definitely adapted much quicker than mine.

Even just understanding the way his brain worked helped him to take control and make changes for himself. This allowed him to move away from the negative outlook that had taken over and to develop new positive patterns instead.

It made me think about just how important it is to have this information when we are young so that the patterns aren't given a chance to become hard-wired into the brain in the first place.

Sadly as I searched for child friendly information it became clear that although there was an abundance for resources out there in regards to self healing it was predominately focused on adults.

Passionate that our young people are empowered with same knowledge strategies and skills I decided to create something especially for them.

My Great Big Positive Life Journal puts together the principles of Growth Mindset, Positive Psychology & Mindfulness in a friendly way to show them that by creating their own positive daily habits now they can support their mental health and wellbeing in the future.

And the feedback has been incredible. It has been completely overwhelming to know we are having an impact on young peoples lives.

Be it from one teenager who is being kinder to themselves and growing in confidence to another who is now able engage in education again for the first time in a long time. Practitioners using the journal with their clients and getting great results to a father telling me that he has become a much better parent as he has worked through the journal with his son. It fills my heart with joy knowing the difference it's making.

Alongside this amazing feedback I have also received many requests for me to produce a journal especially for parents so they to can go on their own personal development journey and work alongside their kids as they go through theirs.

It's wonderful to know that so many parents are wanting to connect with themselves and their kids in this way.

Although a specific journal for parents is something that we are considering for the future I thought why not bring you the information that changed my life on a personal level and as a parent.

Although this book can be used as a stand alone, the main purpose of it is to help you understand the principles so you can support or work alongside your children and as such I have included everything that is in the Superstar Edition for you.

You can just read the book or you may prefer to grab a notebook or blank journal to use as you go through.

Journalling has become increasingly popular in recent years, possibly as we crave space and time away from all the tech we are surrounded with. There's definitely something about putting pen to paper that allows us to fully express ourselves and connect deeply with our thoughts and feelings.

It will also show your kids that you are with them on this journey of self awareness, healing and care and that you are taking the time for some self care of your own.

I hope that you will be left feeling empowered by the end and confident going forward to make the changes you feel will allow you and your family to lead your very own Great Big Positive Life.

Happy reading

Lorna Park

PART 1 POSITIVITY BOOSTS & DAILY HABITS

Section 1: Have an Attitude of Gratitude

This first section is all about the practice of Gratitude. I have decided to leave it practically word for word as written in the journal. Obviously it is age appropriate but the principles are the same for all ages.

"The single Greatest thing you can do to change your life today, would be to start being grateful for what you have right now. And the more grateful you are, the more you will have to be Grateful for."

Oprah Winfrey

Start and end each day with a grateful heart.

Let's be clear, leading a great big positive life isn't some fluffy "oh let's just be positive all the time" kind of thing.

It's not about pretending that everything is great and that we are in a happy place every second of the day.

If anything, it's the opposite. It's about understanding that we WILL have challenges in our lives but knowing that we are capable of facing up to them.

It's about working hard on our self belief, building our confidence and tackling our fears head on. It's about becoming a strong, resilient person, armed with a deep understanding of ourselves and being courageous enough to stay true to who we are.

It's about understanding how we feel. It's knowing that it's ok to be frightened, anxious, sad, angry and frustrated, but not letting these emotions overwhelm us and stop us from moving forward.

It's about being kind to ourselves and others. It's knowing that everyone is different and unique, but equal, and equally deserving of understanding and respect.

It's about having really big goals and dreams and being persistent enough to achieve them.

It's about deciding that we want to lead a happy positive life and understanding that if we work hard enough on ourselves, we can.

If you want to become a happier person the number one place to start is to fill your heart with gratitude. (gratitude...the quality of being thankful)

Focusing on being grateful for the things that are important in your life will lead you to finding so many more things to be grateful for.

If you fill your heart and head with grateful thoughts there won't be space for thoughts about what you don't have, or things that others have, in other words... less space for negative thoughts.

Being grateful gives you an immediate boost. Just thinking of something that is special to you, or saying thank you to someone for the kind thing they did, releases a hormone in your brain that gives you an instant feeling of positivity... The Happiness Hormone (serotonin)

Top Tip - Happiness can't be bought

You might not be feeling happy just now, you might be thinking "I don't have anything to feel grateful for" or "yes I know, I will be grateful when I get my new phone" or " I'll be grateful when my mum gets my that computer game I wanted."

Use the top tip that possessions in the long run won't bring you happiness (there are lots of rich people who look like they have a fabulous life who are thoroughly miserable) and try to look for things in your life, however small, that you can be grateful for.

E.g. The sun was shining today, and you were able to get outside. Your big brother let you into his room and was nice to you, (for a change) your teacher said your worked really hard in class.

The great thing about gratitude's is that they are easy to

find (if you look for them) they never run out and they cost nothing.

Try it now...close your eyes, take a deep breath and when you breathe out say to yourself...

I am so grateful for....................

Dream Space

Struggling to think of things to be grateful for? Try taking time to have some dream space. Another word for dream space can be meditation. This is where you take some time to relax and just be in your thoughts.

Why don't you give it a go now?

Lie on the floor or your bed or sit with your feet planted on the ground and your hands loosely on your knees. Close your eyes and let yourself drift off into a space in your head that is a lovely place.

Let yourself have think about the people in your life that mean the most to you. Relax your body as you feel connected to this happy place.

Imagine you are outside, in a park or at the beach. You might be at home, wherever you enjoy being the most, just be calm in your own thoughts.

Being aware of all that is around you, take a few minutes and think about what you can see, what you can hear and what you can smell.

Think about how you feel, what in the world means the most to you. Is it your family, your friends or where you live? Just try to appreciate all that is around you.

After you have had a few minutes of clearing your mind and visualising all that is important to you try writing 3 things that you are grateful for right now.

Daily Habits

So now that we know being grateful is good for us and gives us a positivity boost of happy hormones the next stage is to make this a daily habit.

Daily habits are so important as you retrain your brain to become more positive.

The best way to keep these positive vibes going is to have a daily practice of writing down at least three things that have happened throughout your day that you are grateful for.

You might find that before bed is the best time to start writing your gratitude's down. That way you will you be able to reflect on all the great things that have happened during your day and it also means that you go off to sleep feeling positive and grateful.

Even on a really bad day there will hopefully be at least one thing that you can find to be grateful for.

There are people that have found that writing down gratitude's every night in a gratitude journal have helped them get through really tough times in their lives.

Reflection (ask yourself...)

My understanding of gratitude is?

Being grateful can make a difference to how I feel?In what way?

What do I feel most grateful for?

In the actual journal there is an updated yearly planner at the back. Each day has space to write down daily gratitudes. It is important to keep practising gratitude's daily, so for you a notebook or gratitude journal is a great place to keep them all.

Section 2: Affirmations

"It's the repetition of affirmations that leads to belief, and once that belief becomes a deep conviction, great things begin to happen."

Muhammad Ali
Elite athlete, Philosopher and

the greatest boxer of all time

For me affirmations has been one of the practices that has changed my life. Each morning my anxiety caused me to wake up with a sick feeling in my stomach and by the time I got up I was so full of stress hormones it was impacting me physically.

Each day now before I get up I use specific affirmations (or mantras as I call them) that I have developed to reset my brain into believing what I want it to believe. I was really surprised how powerful this practice could be and I would encourage anyone that is suffering from anxiety or stress to make using them a priority.

Again below is what I have included within the journal. It gives you an understanding of why affirmations are worthy of including as a daily habit but you might want to create age appropriate ones for yourself.

I Can I Will I Am

Our second instant positive booster is the practice of affirmations.

An "affirmation" is a word used to describe a statement that affirms a belief (confirms the belief to be true).

E.g. I can do it, I am a hard worker, I am strong.

Saying something over and over again will allow your brain to believe what you are saying and the more you say it the more positive about yourself you will become.

How do you talk to yourself?

Do you think you are positive about yourself or negative?

E.g. If you make a mistake what is the first thing you would say to yourself? Something like... "oh how dumb!" ?

Do you believe in yourself or do you tell yourself that you can't do certain things?

You wouldn't be alone; most people have negative thoughts first.

We will go into more detail later regarding self-belief and self-talk but for now try and give it a go.

It may take some practice and you might feel a bit silly shouting out things like...

"I am great" "I will work hard" "I am brave" "I am good" "I am kind to others"

Don't over think it... Just do it!

You don't need to shout them out either., just repeat them over and over again. Try practicing in a mirror and tell yourself

"I am positive" "I am happy" "I believe in me" "I always try my best" "I love my life."

E.g. Let's say you have a project to do and you have to stand up in front of the class and talk. You feel really nervous, scared even, then try repeating over and over again "I am a great talker" "I speak well in front of my class" "I am confident" "I love a challenge" "Bring it on !"

Affirmations are a sure-fire way to make you feel great and install some self-belief if you are lacking it.

Now, once you have said them, try writing them down. In fact sometimes it's easier to write them down first and then repeat them over and over.

Think of a situation you have been in where you have not felt confident. How did you feel? What did you want to do?

Then think of some affirmations that could help you in that situation.

Daily Habits

Just as we are doing with our Gratitude's try doing the same with your Affirmations and start to let them become a daily habit.

Daily habits are so important. We are much more prone to have negative thoughts than we are positive, so we have to make a conscious decision to have positive thoughts. Practicing every day will confirm the positive beliefs and that then starts to retrain the brain towards a more positive and confident you.

Just as Gratitude's are great to do before bed, Affirmations are often great to do in the morning to help you start your day off right.

Try waking up tomorrow and starting your day off by repeating...

"I am awake" "I feel great" "I am ready for the day ahead" "I will work hard today" "I can achieve anything I put my mind to""I love my life" "Whoooo Hoooo" "Bring on the day !!!"

Top Tip - Try writing your favourite affirmations onto some sticky notes and put them up where you can see them everyday. e.g. beside your bed, or in the inside of your pencil case. This will remind you to say your affirmations everyday. Different affirmations work for different things. Mix them up depending how your are feeling.

Reflection

What can I use affirmations for?

How do I feel after saying my daily affirmations?

What difference do I think it will make if I do affirmations regularly, long term?

Let your day, start in the right way by really appreciating just how wonderful and special you really are. Knowing your true worth doesn't have to mean that you are obnoxious or overly cocky. Loving yourself, without ego will give you the confidence to go out there and rule the world.

PART ONE
GROWTH MINDSET

At the very beginning of my self development journey I came across a book that blew my mind. It was called Mindset by Dr Carol Dweck. It was this book that allowed me to see what was going on in my son's head and that the main reason he was becoming anxious, stressed out and giving up on everything was because he had a fixed mindset.

It is also where I came across the word Neuroplasticity, after which my world would never be the same again.

I made my husband read it immediately and it was from this book that we implemented many of the changes we made as a family. Praise was one of the main ones and hand on heart I still can't quite believe the massive impact just praising our kids in a slightly different way could have on their outlook, self esteem and confidence.

The Yellow Brick Road of Blessings

The yellow brick road is from the famous film The Wizard of Oz. Dorothy is lost in Oz and is needing help from the Great Wizard, so she can get home. She is told to follow the yellow brick road to Kansas City where the all-powerful wizard will be able to grant her her wish of returning home.

On her way she meets three characters: "The Scarecrow" "The Tin Man" and "The Lion".

Each of them thinks they need help. The Scarecrow thinks he's stupid and dreams of having a brain, the Tin Man thinks he can't fall in love and dreams of having a heart and the Lion thinks he is a big scaredy cat and dreams of possessing some courage.

Dorothy decides to take them with her as she believes the Wizard will make their dreams come true.

When they get to Kansas the Wizard sets them a challenge

and says that they will only get their wishes if they manage to kill the "Wicked Witch of the East".

During this challenge they all get more than they bargained for. Without them realising it, they start to develop the very things they think they are missing.

The Scarecrow has to think quickly and smartly and therefore uses his brain, the Tin Man shows he has compassion and kindness and in fact already has a heart and the Lion has to get brave to protect them all, so isn't cowardly after all.

Their journey along the yellow brick road was actually a journey of self-discovery. (learning about who they were)

Oprah Winfrey

In her last ever TV show of "The Oprah Winfrey Show", Oprah Winfrey talks about her journey through her 25 years and over 4500 episodes, as her "yellow brick road of blessings"

The yellow brick road is her path through the past 25years of self-discovery on the show and the blessings are all the fantastic things that have happened and people she has met along the way.

But who is Oprah Winfrey and why is her story such an inspirational one to tell?

Oprah Winfrey is one of the most famous women in the world. She ran her own successful TV show for over 25 years and was the first African American to make over a billion dollars. She is also known for being inspirational, kind, and an activist for human rights especially for under-privileged young black women and the LGBT community.

She is a hugely admired black woman of power and influence. She was the first black person in America to rank in the top 50 most generous Americans', and by 2004 it was reported that she had given away approx. $400 million of her own personal wealth to educational causes.

Her TV show was known for tackling difficult subjects like racism, addiction, abuse, Lesbian and Gay rights, in a time when these subjects where not really discussed openly on television. With viewers totalling over 48 million per week she paved the way for a much more open and accepting society within broadcasting. In a world dominated by white men she stood up as a proud black woman and smashed through barriers like no other.

But her life had not always been like this, for Oprah was born into an extremely poor family and had a really difficult childhood. Her parents were teenagers and unmarried which in the 1950's was looked upon extremely badly and she spent her first years with her grandmother in extreme poverty.

Her grandmother dressed her in hessian overalls made from potato sacks, for which she was cruelly taunted by other children, and her toys were dolls made out of corn on the cobs.

Her grandmother taught her to read by the time she was

three, so she could learn to read the bible in church, and she was known for standing up in church and reciting her passages in a loud and clear voice, giving her the nickname "the preacher".

Although they were extremely poor and times hard, Oprah adored her grandmother and talks of the fond memories that she has of this hard-working woman and her time spent with her, stating that it was her grandmother who had encouraged her to speak in public and who "gave me a positive sense of myself".

Sadly, though for Oprah things were to get a lot worse when, at the age of 9 she went to live with her mother. Her mother worked as a housemaid and was not around much of the time and Oprah was left with family members who beat her and abused her. Not surprisingly her behaviour deteriorated and after turning into an extremely difficult teenager, at the age of 14 she was sent to a juvenile detention home.

So how on earth did Oprah manage to become one of the most successful women in the world?

Oprah attributes going to live with her father, a strict disciplinarian, for the turnaround in her life.

Although strict, he was encouraging and made her education a priority, noted for making her read a book a week and asking for a report once she had finished.

Quickly she changed from a difficult teenage tearaway to a high flying honours student. She secured her a full scholarship to Tennessee State University where she studied communication.

At the age of 17 she entered and won a beauty pageant and as part of her prize she visited a local radio station who, for fun, let her read the news. So impressed by her warm voice and ability to read so well in public they hired her on the spot, and she worked part time during her last year of high school and first couple of years at college.

Things moved quickly from there and after graduating University she became the first black news reader in Nashville. Television soon awaited and her rise from news reporter to local TV host, to National broadcaster happened in the period of just a few years.

Oprah's TV show dominated the world of talk shows for 25 years and although she hung up her hat in 2011 she still owns a TV Network, appears in many other shows and also has a big film career.

Oprah's motto in life is "Be your best self". Not one for using her past as an excuse for not going out there and grabbing life, she attributes her difficult start for building up her courage, and resilience in life to become successful, dismissing the wealth she has created as unimportant and telling her viewers on the last episode...

"I listened and grew, and I know you grew with me. Sometimes I was the teacher and more often than not you taught me". Going on to say "so that's what we learnt on this show, you are responsible for your life and when you understand that, everything changes my friends, so don't wait for somebody else to fix you, to save you or complete you..."

If you look at your life as "a yellow brick road of blessings" and focus on all the great things that happen along the way, don't you think you would find yourself a much more positive person with a happier outlook?

SECTION 1: WHAT IS GROWTH MINDSET

"Effort is one of those things that gives meaning to life. Effort means you care about something, that it is important to you and you are willing to work for it."

Dr Carol Dweck
Professor, Psychologist, and the person
who brought growth mindset into our lives.

Growth Mindset - Science Heads

Did you know that your brain has millions of nerve cells called Neurones?

These Neurones connect with one another and they control your movements and your thoughts.

It was once thought that after early childhood these cells stopped growing and connecting, and that once you reached about 7 your brain was fully developed and your basic level of intelligence and ability for things was pretty much fixed for life.

More recently research has shown that this is not the case, and through effort and learning you can grow more neurones and the connections can get stronger, making you more intelligent and more able.

If you think of the brain as a muscle, the harder you work the bigger and stronger it will become.

The world of neuroscience has a name for it.

"Neuroplasticity"

The ability of the brain to change through focus, effort and learning.

So we know the "Neuro" bit is the nerve cells in your brain. Think of the "plasticity" part, like plastic the brain can be moulded and shaped through stimulating it with lots of learning and effort. Intense effort speeds up the process.

When you work really hard at something you might say, "oh my head hurts." Imagine that's the feeling of all the neurones connecting making the brain stronger.

If you believe that you just have a certain amount intelligence (e.g. for math's) or ability (e.g. talent for sport) and no matter how hard you work your level of intelligence will stay the same, then that is called a "FIXED MINDSET".

Through the next section we will look at why having a fixed mindset can lead you easily give up on things, lose your confidence and not fulfil your potential and how moving to a "GROWTH MINDSET" can help you grow your intelligence, grow your skills and your self-belief.

So what is a growth mindset?

Growth Mindset is the understanding that you can develop your abilities and intelligence. It is the belief that you can get smarter and that effort makes you stronger.

Having a growth Mindset will lead you to focus more on learning, put in the extra time and effort and allow you to be more willing to learn from your mistakes.

Here are some differences between fixed and growth mindsets.

Someone with a fixed mindset might say...

"I want to look smart, I don't want anyone to think that I'm stupid."

Someone with a growth mindset might say...

"I want to look smart and I know that I can get smarter if I work at it."

Lets look at the difference between mindsets Growth Mindset V's Fixed Mindset

Inspired by Dr Reid Wilson

Fixed Mindset

I am either good at something or I am not!

When I get frustrated, I will most likely give up.

I hate challenges; challenges scare me.

When I make a mistake, I show my weaknesses and that I am no good.

It makes me feel good when I am told that I am smart.

I don't like it when others around me do well as it makes me feel like a failure.

My ability is what matters and determines the outcome.

With a Growth Mindset you are more likely to say.

With hard work and effort I can learn anything I want to.

When I get frustrated, I keep going and persevere.

I like to challenge myself whenever possible, because if something is too easy I'm not learning.

Making mistakes helps me learn.

It makes me feel good when I am told I have tried hard.

I love it when others around me do well, it makes me feel inspired.

Putting in effort and having a great attitude determines a successful outcome.

What can I say to myself

Instead of, Try saying

I'm not good at this.

What am I missing?

I'm awesome at this

I'm on the right track.

I give up.

I'll use some of the strategies I've learnt.

This is too hard.

This may take some time and effort.

I can't make this any better.

I can always improve, so I'll keep trying.

I just can't do Math's.

I'm going to train my brain in Math's.

I made a mistake.

Mistakes help me learn better.

She's so smart, I'll never be that smart

I'm going to figure out how she does it.

It's good enough

Is it really my best work?

Plan "A" didn't work

Good thing the alphabet has 25 more letters.

" If parents want to give their children a gift, the best this they can do is to teach their children to love challenges, be intrigued by mistakes, enjoy effort, and keep on learning. That way, their children don't need to be salves to praise. They will have a lifelong way to build and repair their own confidence. "

Dr Carol Dweck
Growth Mindset Queen

Praise

Now we all love to be praised, it makes us feel good and that we are doing something right. Praise is such an important part of life but often they way we are praised for certain things can put us into either a fixed or growth mindset.

Look how praise can do this...

Praising **high intelligence/ high** ability can cause you to have a fixed mindset.

"Wow, you are really smart. Well done for getting 10 to of 10 for that test"

or

Wow, you are so talented at dancing. You smashed that exam. Well done I'm so proud"

Now see what can happen when things get tough...It's time for the next test and the next dancing exam.

Look how the way praise was given for **ability** has affected their mindset

"Ok it's time for the next test, what if I don't get 10 out 10, they won't think I'm smart anymore. I'm stressed, I feel sick, I don't want to do this, I can't do this."

"Ok this class has been way harder than the last one, the next exam is going to be so tough, I'm not sure I'm going to do well. All these dancers are way better than me there is no point in me trying as I'm just going got fail and if I fall they won't think I'm such a good dancer."

Praising **effort** instead of ability, can help create a growth mindset.

"Wow, you worked so hard to achieve that 10 out of 10. Well done, your effort has really paid off. I'm so proud of you"; or

"Wow, I'm so proud of al that effort you've put into your dancing. Your results reflect all that hard work. It was so worth all these extra hours of sweat and sore legs. I'm so so proud of you well done."

Look how praising **effort** makes a difference.

"So the next test is coming up; I'm a bit worried but if I work doubly hard and I don't do very well, mum and dad will still be proud of me for really giving it a go."

"Wow, this class is at another level. Passing the next exam is going to be so tough. Look at all these dancers, they are amazing, I'm going to have to get down to it straight away if I want to be as good as them. I really want to reach the next grade so I'm going to have to watch what they do and work as hard as them. Mum and dad have been so supportive of all my efforts I'm sure that will be happy to bring me to a few extra classes...I really want this."

Can you see how praise can set you spinning into either a fixed or a growth mindset. It is not just how you see yourself but how others see you that can affect you too.

Do you recognise any of this in yourself?

Are you seeing the differences between having a growth mindset and a fixed one now.

Your mindset really does affect your behaviour and at the end of the day your overall achievements.

People with fixed mindsets when they encounter obstacles tend to give up easily, as that believe they don't have what it takes to learn hard things, or that they mustn't have been as clever or able as they had first thought.

People with growth mindsets tend to relish challenges and understand the value of practicing. they see effort as the only way to success.

Please don't miss this opportunity to grow your brain by thinking "I can't do it' "It's too hard" or "It's too much work"

In the long run just enjoy the learning process, have more fun with it, go of challenges and interesting tasks in order to learn even more.

The love of learning is such an amazing thing to have in your life and will lead you to places you never thought possible.

It will take a bit of effort and time to retrain your brain from a fixed mindset to a growth one and the further you go toward adulthood the harder it becomes, so now is the time to get to it.

LIFE LESSONS AND INSPIRING - STORIES NO2

TRUE STORY - CHARLIE PARK

Charlie was really good at judo. He had a natural talent for it. He showed this talent very quickly, and he flew through his first few grades.

His parents were very proud of him, they kept telling him how great he was and how much talent he had for the sport. This made Charlie feel great... He loved judo!

Charlie was wanting to take his judo to the next level and even talked about one day doing it at a professional level. So, he started competitions with his club. He would come home with medals and trophies and he felt great about himself. Everyone was so proud and happy for him.

His coach thought he was doing so well that he should move up to the next class. Charlie was so excited and so were his parents, but this is where it all started to change.

Everyone in the class was really good, Charlie was no longer flipping people over with ease. It was taking loads of effort and it was hard. Charlie was starting to wonder if he was quite as good at this as he had first thought.

Next came competition time. Charlie's mum was so excited as she hadn't been at the previous one and couldn't wait to see him in action. Unusually Charlie was very quiet as the competition was getting started.

The first round was tough, and he got beaten. He was really deflated, but his parents told him to keep going.

"Come on" they said "you can do this, you're really good"

Charlie was not feeling that he was really good...

In the second round he got hurt and he didn't look like he was enjoying himself very much. He was better than his opponent and did manage to beat him and win a point for his team, but his head was going down and he let getting hurt really affect him.

Round three, and Charlie managed to scrape through and win a second point for his team, but he was not happy. It just wasn't as easy as he thought it was going to be, he started to lose his confidence and he didn't even want to do the fourth and final round.

Of course, what happened in that round, he got absolutely floored!

His opponent had much more experience than him, but that didn't matter to Charlie he was devastated and felt like a failure.

The fact that the two points he had won gave his team an overall victory, didn't even make a difference. He just felt terrible and he couldn't understand why anyone had told him he was talented at judo. Couldn't they see that just wasn't the case.

Over the next few weeks Charlie started to take a while to get ready for training. His mum would be shouting "come on, we've got to go" over and over again. He would get stressed and not feel well and when he did get to training, he just didn't even try.

His parents kept telling him to work hard and do his best and that he was really good, but now Charlie saw this as pressure because he didn't believe a word of it. He felt like he was letting everyone down because they had thought he was great, and he wasn't.

Charlie decided to give up judo. He just didn't want to do it anymore.

Mum and dad told him they were so disappointed, as he could have been so good. Charlie took this as disappointed *in* him rather than disappointed *for* him, and he felt even worse, but he knew he had made the right decision to give up, because this way they wouldn't find out that he was actually not really good after all.

The problem for Charlie was that he believed his success at judo depended on what talent he had for it. He had done pretty well but when it started to get tough and take effort he started to believe he wasn't very talented after all. So he lost his love for it and in the long run, lost out.

On the other hand,...

Charlie loved playing football with his friends, he really wanted to join a club and although his mum and dad didn't particularly think he had that much natural talent for it they let him go along.

They were worried about encouraging him as they didn't want him to face disappointment.

"You're going to have to work really hard if you want to get better" they would say... **"It's going to take lots of effort and practise."**

Charlie knew there was a Sunday league team in his year group, so he set himself the goal of getting into the team and he got down to work.

His parents were really worried that his dream might not become a reality but told him to keep going, not give up and work really hard.

"Well, you're going to have to put everything you've got into this, every practise, every game, work on your skills, and if you work really, really hard then you never know."

When he had club matches they noticed the effort he put in and praised him for all his hard work. They told him how proud they were off him or sticking at it and how they could see his improvement.

The harder he worked and the more he practised, the better he got.

Charlie's confidence began to grow. He worked hard at every training session, he worked on his skill, he watched loads of training videos of the best players in the world.

When he got the chance to train with the Sunday league team, although worried that they were all better than him, he used the experience to learn as much as he could from them.

He didn't worry that the coaches might think he wasn't very good compared to the rest of them. He knew by now if he wanted to improve he had to keep going and work really hard.

Every training session he was all over it and as time went on he got better and better and better.

And it was noticed...

The coaches had started talking about how hard he was working, how he was always there for his team, how every game he put in the most effort, and now they were beginning to talk about how good he was...

Charlie could see that it wasn't just down to his basic talent for the game but that, if he wanted something badly enough and he was willing to work for it, then he could improve and ultimately succeed.

Charlie is now playing Sunday League football but more importantly because he has a growth mindset, he didn't just stop and think **"yeah I made it"** he is working harder than ever before.

If he slips up, he doesn't let it affect him, he learns from it and moves on. If he gets the chance to play with more experienced players, he relishes it and gets inspired by them.

At matches he doesn't just want to play easy teams and beat them, he wants to play the really good teams and win, lose or draw he knows that with every game, every training session, every challenge, every defeat, there is always something to learn and improve on.

He believes in himself, his confidence has grown, his determination is at an all them high and he will never give up!

And the best bit...

He loves the game even more than he could've possibly imagined.

His parents are prouder of him than he may ever know. To see their son work so hard, be persistent, take knock backs on the chin and be so passionate about the game, fills them with joy and happiness.

Most importantly Charlie is proud of himself, his dedication, learning, effort and hard work is paying off and he knows this is just the beginning.

This growth mindset that Charlie has developed has not only affected his football but, because he understands it, he is able to apply it to the different areas of his life, such as learning guitar, working on tricky subjects at school and how he views the world in general.

Can you see how Charlie's mindset was completely different in football than judo? How he was affected by his own idea of ability/ talent and his parent's idea about ability/talent.

How they praised him differently when they thought he had a natural talent for judo versus what they thought about his football skills.

Hopefully you can see that having a growth mindset can help you succeed and you understand that if you put in the effort, practise and keep going you will improve, be it at judo, football, guitar, math's, reading, art, English, dancing, swimming or anything that you choose to put your mind too.

(Incase you were wondering who Charlie Park is, he is our son and the reason we want you all to know about growth mindset and how it can change your world.)

Try having a conversation with your loved ones about praise and see if they would be prouder of your ability or your efforts.

Explain what you have been reading about and learning and ask them to help you to achieve more by encouraging your hard work and effort over your natural ability for things.

By having this conversation, you may be opening their eyes up to the benefits of having a growth mindset.

It's all down to you!

At the end of the day you are the only person who can determine how you deal with situations and you are the only one that can decide if you are going to move forward with a growth mindset or a fixed one.

You are the only one that can decide if you are going to let how others praise you, or view your talents in certain areas effect how you feel about yourself.

Achieving something that has taken a lot of hard work actually makes us feel even better about ourselves than achieving something that was easy.

So go on, get out there, challenge yourself and make yourself proud!

Reflection

What does having a Growth Mindset mean to me?

Why would having a Growth Mindset be beneficial to me?

The areas of my life I would like to have a growth mindset are?

What will I need to change about myself to continue to have a Growth Mindset?

What Fixed Mindset things do I say to myself on a regular basis and what can I say to myself instead?

What new thing would I love to learn, knowing what I know now about Growth Mindset?

Hopefully you will now have decided that

having a growth mindset going forward is the best way to go, the next 4 sections will give you lots of help in achieving this... they include, goal setting, persistence is key, the power of YET and how to make friends with failure.

SECTION 2 - "YOU AIN'T NOTHING BUT A GOAL DIGGER"

Goals are something that I have always used to motivate myself. For me unless I have a goal board and a sticky note wall plan nothing would ever get done.

Encouraging our kids from an early age to set their own goals can make a massive difference when they begin to face their own challenges. If they are in the habit of setting goals and breaking them down then they can see that what might have seemed impossible to achieve can now become achievable.

"People with goals succeed because they know where they are going..."

Earl Nightingale
Motivational Speaker, Author and American Marine.
One of 15 survivors from the battleship USS Arizona
during the attack on Pearl Harbour WW11

Goal Setting

Believe or not Goal Setting is one of the best ways for you to, not only keep developing your growth mindset, but also a really great way for you to work on your Internal Motivation (also known as Intrinsic Motivation). Intrinsic means, personal, internal, essential, built in. Motivation is the reason behind why you do something.

What this really means is that you can motivate yourself to do something for your own personal reward, e.g. you just really enjoyed the challenge.

Think of praising yourself for the effort and determination you showed in completing the task, or the fact that you practiced really hard and got better....well done you !

Imagine how successful you could be if you didn't rely on other people's responses to you to motivate you.

Praise and recognition from parents, teachers and eventually bosses would be the icing on the cake and always lovely to receive, but not something that would drive you forward.

If we care and are driven forward by the good stuff (praise) then that can also mean that we can give up or are stopped in our tracks by the bad stuff. (criticism)

Imagine the power in being completely independent in your belief of yourself and your ability to develop your skills and intelligence through hard work and effort.

Being able to motivate yourself means that when you are praised for your ability, it won't send you spinning into a fixed mindset where you believe you have a set amount of ability or intelligence for something, thus setting you on the downwards spiral of self-belief.

Remember with a fixed mindset when things get tough you can start to believe you are not good enough, rather than believing that you can improve, grow and get better if you practice. So, put in the effort and don't give up.

Working towards having a strong Intrinsic Motivation will help you to become stronger, more resilient, more confident, more driven and in the long run will give you better results.

In order to set effective goals it is important to understand that there is a future and not everything has to happen right this second.

When you are young you just want things to happen there and then. You want that new toy, your favourite sweet, you're excited, you can't wait you have to have it!

Having an understanding that everything in life is not going to happen like that for you is such a valuable lesson and will really benefit you in the future.

Learn the skills now to be patient, to take your time, to see the long game...

Take the sweet test.

You are offered your favourite sweet. You are like OMG I need that sweet, I love that sweet, I want that sweet!

What if you are told you can have this sweet right now or if you wait till tomorrow you can have the whole packet?

What would you do?

This might seem silly but if you grow up without having to have instant gratification (the desire to experience pleasure or fulfilment immediately) then you are much more likely to see things through, not give up and pursue the things that you want to succeed in.

Instant gratification versus delayed gratification

We live in a world where lots of things are instant. With social media for instance we can upload photos instantly and get feedback instantly from our followers/friends.

Our brains are pretty wired to want things instantly and there is a reason for it. If we feel hungry, we want to eat, if we feel thirsty, we want to drink (it's about survival).

So, what is delayed gratification?

Delayed gratification is the ability to put off something mildly fun or pleasurable now, in order to gain something that is more fun, pleasurable, or rewarding, later.

Resisting short-term reward in favour of a longer-term reward requires you to be able to understand and visualise future.

If you set your own GOALS then only you are responsible for them. It's up to you, if you are willing to do whatever it takes to achieve them.

You may have heard of **SMART** goals before, this is where each letter in the word smart means something.

SMART GOALS

S meaning Specific or Stretching, (you stretch yourself to achieve it)

M meaning Measurable or Meaningful, (you can measure the outcome)

A meaning Achievable, (not something out of reach)

R meaning Realistic or Rewarding, (that is doable but will make you feel good)

T meaning Time based or Trackable, (you set a time that you want to achieve it by)

Smart goals are an excellent way of giving you focus when writing your goals and it's definitely recommended that your goals include all the words associated with the smart method. But how about we step it up another level?

How about we become **EPIC.**

EPIC is probably a word that you know well, meaning something is really really great, and setting EPIC goals can be lots of fun as they take you to a place where you have to really think about what each goal means to you personally and deeply.

EPIC goals are something that we learnt from an incredible lady, Positive Psychologist, Niyc Pidgeon.

She inspires us to take things up a level, to stretch ourselves and when it comes to EPIC goals she believes that you would be much better setting yourself a couple of really epic goals than lots of goals that are wishy washy and that you can easily give up on.

EPIC GOALS

E. stands for Excited. (If your goal makes you excited, it will motivate you and bring out positive emotions, and positive emotions are something that we all want to have).

P. stands for Purpose. (What is the purpose of this goal? Does it connect you to your ultimate goal? Having a purpose is the same as having a reason why you are doing it, so think about, what is your reason WHY?).

I. stands for Intuition. (Take your head out of it for a moment. Do you feel it from your heart? Where does your goal actually come from? Does it push you forward? Does it challenge you and stretch you?)

C. stands for Committed. (Are you really committed to making this goal happen? If not, then it doesn't come from a place of deep thinking. You have to be true to yourself and really think about what it is you want to achieve.)

There is definitely no wrong or right when it comes to EPIC goals, they just have to mean something really important and special to you.

Try writing an EPIC goal for yourself. Just one to start with and then you can start to think of some more.

Sometimes it's easier to break down your goals. Starting at the top with one the one Big EPIC Goal you want to achieve and then working backwards underneath using smaller EPIC goals that will help you achieve this.

Lots of little epic goals can add up to one massive achievement.

Remember to give yourself a massive well done as you complete each epic goal that moves you forward.

Create yourself a goal board

Creating a goal board is a fun and easy way to help you stick to your goals. Being able to see your goals visually will inspire you.

Get a board approx. 60cm by 40cm (Board can be very strong card or cork boards are great)

Sellotape, scissors, blu tac, pins (if using cork board)

Magazines, photos, inspiring quotes,

Pens, Markers, Paper.

Tip: if you are using strong card wrapping it in cellophane will protect the card and you will be able to stick everything on with blu tac. That way when you come to change your board you will be able to do it easily.

Take your time, lay out all the things you want on your goal board in front of you, before you start so you have a clear vision of what you want it to look like.

Your board doesn't need to just reflect your goals it can also be used as a vision board for how you want to feel, so you can mix it up a bit. Look up some quotes that relate to how you want to feel.

If you want to feel empowered then look up empowerment quotes, if you want to feel happy, look up quotes for happiness, the same for success, then print them.

Look up and cut out picture in magazines that relate to you goal. If you are wanting to learn to swim, print off a pic that represents that to you. It doesn't need to be of a swimmer, it could be of a hotel with a great pool that you would like to be able to swim in.

If one of your goals is to learn a foreign language, then a photo of the country the language is from would be great.

There are no rules to what your goal is or what pictures you use to represent these goals to you. That's the beauty of it, your goal board will be as individual as you are.

If you fancy getting really creative, then why not draw your now inspirational quotes and pictures for each of your goals.

Arrange all your pics on the floor before you attach them to your board to make sure you are happy with the lay out.

Lastly attach your pics, then get some paper and write the dates you want to complete your goal by, cut them out and stick them on.

Don't forget to date all your goals to keep you on track.

Goal Board Complete!!!

3,2,1, ACTION

There is absolutely no point in spending time setting yourself lots of goals and then not taking the action in order to achieve them. Having a goal with no action is just a dream at the end of the day, so it is up to you if you choose to take the action required.

Hopefully if you have followed the process of setting goals that really mean something to you, then you will be inspired to stop dreaming and start doing.

Whereas a goal/vision board can bring your hopes and dreams to life, just looking at your beautiful creation is not going to suddenly make these dreams and goals come true. Now is the time to get to work and take responsibility for your goals.

"The secret of getting ahead is getting started."

Mark Twain
Author

Reflection

Why do I think having a goal is important?

Why do I think it important to put a timescale on my goals?

When I write myself a goal what do I hope to achieve?

Do I think goals should be fun and why?

What are the things I should consider when setting a goal?

Once I have set my goal what must I do next?

SECTION 3 - PERSISTENCE IS KEY: "DON'T QUIT"

"I hated every minute of training, but I said, don't quit. Suffer now and live the rest of your life as a Champion!"

Muhammad Ali
The greatest boxing
champion of the world

Persistence is key

Remember how we talked about the brain having millions of neurones (nerve cells) and how they connect together through learning, effort and hard work? Well, the more you keep challenging your brain the more connections you will make, and your brain will become stronger and stronger.

If you keep going and are persistent especially with things that are difficult, the stronger and stronger these connections become and the things that you once found difficult become easier to achieve.

The harder you try, the more motivated you are, the more alert you are m the bigger the change in your brain.

If you focus intensely on a task and are determined to make it happened the brain releases special chemicals which enable it to change, and for you to learn new skills.

" If you really want to do something you'll find a way, if you don't, you'll find an excuse"

Jim Rohn
Incredible business man, trainer
and motivational speaker.

What do we do when we see a baby learning to walk? Do we laugh at them or think they are stupid for falling down? Of course, we don't. We encourage them for trying so hard, we praise them for all their effort and we help them achieve their goal.

Have you ever seen a baby after they have fallen down a hundred times give up and think to themselves?

"Oh, this is too hard. I think I'm going to just crawl for the rest of my life"

Of course not, they keep trying to build the muscles in their legs, so they have the strength and they build their brain muscle which teaches them how to put one foot in front of another.

Think for a moment about just how many things you had to learn as a baby. My word there's lots isn't there?

Why on earth would we think that suddenly we can no longer develop our brains and our skills.

It's perseverance that that will get you to your end goal, whatever that might be.

So, we know the brain is a muscle, what do we have to do if we want that muscle to get bigger?

That's right, we have to work it out. Just in the same way as a body builder has to work out his body every day to get bigger and stronger, we must continue to keep working out our brains every day to keep it strong and healthy too. It definitely is a matter of **use** it or **lose** it.

Reflection

Being persistent when I want to achieve a goal is vital. What other areas of my life could I be persistent help with?

What does being persistent really mean to me?

Right now, do I have persistence or do I find you give up easily on things? (be honest with yourself)

What things do I give up easily on? (e.g. When you read a

book do I always finish it? When you play a game do you give up if you are losing?)

Is it easier to be persistent if I think I am good or enjoy the challenge?

How will feel if I complete a task that I find challenging?

Try thinking of something that you really find hard to keep going at and think about what you can do to make sure you get the job done.

Next time you face a challenge try your hardest to see it through.

SECTION 4 - THE POWER OF YET

"Realise now the power that your words command, if you simply choose them wisely"

Tony Robbins
The number one motivational
speaker and life coach of all time.

The Power of "yet"

Sometimes the smallest of things can have the biggest impact.

Who would have thought that a word as tiny as "yet" could make such a huge difference in our lives, especially when we are talking about perseverance?

The word yet can stop us from giving up, encourage us to preserve and ultimately help us achieve our goals.

"I can't do it"

"I can't do it yet"

"I can't do it yet, but with effort, hard work and perseverance, I will get there"

From now on every time you come up against something tricky try using the word yet and see where it takes you

"I won't do it" "I won't do it, yet" "I can't do it yet" "I want to do it"

"How do I do it?" "I'll try and do it" "I can do it" I will do it" "Yes, I did it"

Reflection

What does the word YET mean?

How can using the word YET can help me have a growth mindset?

A situation I could use the word YET for is? Does it change the way I feel about that situation?

SECTION 5 - MAKING FRIENDS WITH FAILURE

We all hate to fail at things, I know I certainly did. Shifting my thoughts from a failure being a defeat to something that can teach me something, has really allowed me to break free from my own fear of failing. I would always hold back, not try just incase things went wrong, but the truth is you can't succeed unless you are willing to fail. Changing my view that failing is a negative thing has allowed me try lots of new things in many areas of my life.

We actively encourage failures in our house now. Every night we ask "What did we fail at and what did we learn from it?".

"I have not failed, I've just found 10,000 ways that didn't work"

Thomas A Edison
The inventor of the lightbulb,
record player and motion picture camera,

and probably the biggest failure in the whole world

Making friends with failure

When we have a fixed mindset, the goal is to look smart or talented and we will do anything to make sure no one would think otherwise.

Why would we want to fail right?

Now that you know that you can change you ability through effort then failing can become your friend. You can look at failing completely differently.

"If I fail I will look stupid" can now become "If I fail I can learn from it and in the end I will become smarter"

Just because you fail at something doesn't mean that you walk around with "LOSER" tattooed to your forehead for the rest of your life.

If you are too scared to fail then you will start to be controlled by fear and that is not what the emotion "fear" is intended for (fear is intended to keep you safe!)

Being controlled by the fear of failing will stop you bring new things, will give you an excuse to give up easily and in the long run stop you growing, developing new skills and stop you achieving the amazing new things your newly adopted growth mindset is waiting for you to achieve.

Remember you can change your intelligence/ability though challenges, learning, and putting in effort. If you are too scared to fail then you will never challenge yourself to do anything. Surely it makes more sense for you to try and fail, learn from it, try and fail again, learn from it, try and fail again and learn from it, until you learn all you need to know to achieve your goal.

"Don't worry about failures, worry about all the chances you miss when you don't even try"

Jack Canfield
American Author,
Sold over 100 million copies
of his books worldwide.

"Failure is not in the falling down. Failure is refusing to get back up and trying again"

Chinese Proverb

So, from now on try and look at failure as your best friend. The best kind of friend that will always be there to help you grow.

"I've probably earned the right to screw up a few times. I don't want the fear of failure to stop me from doing what I really care about"

Emma Watson
Hermione from Harry Potter
and all round incredible actress

We can class failure, setbacks, challenges and disappointments in the same bracket.

As you grow older these things become part of daily life. The quicker you can bounce back the easier these setbacks will be to deal with now and into adulthood.

Failures, setbacks, challenges and disappointments make you stronger, much more robust and will help you learn.

Remember, failing at something doesn't make you a failure, but the way you handle it will show you who you are.

"Success is not final, Failure is not fatal, it's the courage to continue that counts"

Winston Churchill
British Prime Minister,
led the country to victory during WWII

Often our feelings can overwhelm us when we fail at something or we face disappointment. It can feel like the end of the world.

Have you ever heard your parents ever say..

"You should be grateful" "You're really lucky, there are starving children in the world"

"You're lucky to have a roof over your head, why are you so disappointed in not.....? (whatever it is)

Well of course it might all be true, but it doesn't take away from the way you feel in that moment. It's good to acknowledge how you feel and then try and put it into context in the bigger picture of life in general. A good way to look at failure/disappointment is to say to yourself.

"Am I going to be crying or worrying about what's happened this time next year"

If the answer is no then take a deep breath, take a moment and try and breathe that failure away.

So from now on encourage failing. The bigger the failure the bigger the lesson you can learn from it.

Experiencing a failure not only allows you to learn from it (which changes and develops your brain) it also allows you to develop different strategies to deal with it, and this will help you in the future, giving you the confidence in you own ability to cope with whatever life throws your way.

Each time you bounce back for a failure the quicker you will be able to bounce back from the next one and easier each failure will become.

Reflection

How do I feel about failing at this time?

Does failing at something worry me? If so why?

What will worrying about failing stop me from doing?

· · ·

How would I feel if I didn't care what other people thought of me? Do I think I would find it easier to fail at things?

How would I feel if I let go of my fears and knew that each time I made a mistake or failed at something I could learn from it, become a more confident person and understand more about myself?

Am I ready to let go of my the fear of failing?

So go out and embrace all the challenges to have coming your way and remember...

"When you learn from defeat you haven't really lost"

Zig Ziglar
A pioneer in the science of human potential.

PART TWO
CHOOSE HAPPY

"Happiness is not something you postpone for the future; it is something that you design for the present."

Jim Rohn
Writer and Motivational Speaker

Hopefully now you can see that we have a large say in how we feel. In fact science has shown that we are in control of 40% of our own happiness (50% being genetic and 10% circumstantial). That said the way our brain works is that patterns are developed based on what we think and how we react to situations. These patterns become deeper the more our brain learns from our thoughts and actions.

Along with the fact that negative thoughts are three times stronger than positive thoughts it makes total sense that we have to make a conscious decision to become more positive in our lives and reset the negative patterns within our brain.

The scientific research that has been done in this area shows us that there are a number of things we can do in order to train our brain to focus on the positive.The next section covers these principles which of course can be put into action at any age.

SECTION 1 - POSITIVE PSYCHOLOGY. THE SCIENCE OF HAPPINESS

SELF-WORTH AND SELF BELIEF

Now you know that you can achieve what you want through hard work determination, persistence and practice. Having a growth mindset will allow you to achieve anything you want in life **but** achieving great things and being successful doesn't automatically mean that you will be happy.

If deep down you don't believe you deserve to be happy and are worthy having a fantastic life, then you will never be able to enjoy all the wonderful things you have achieved or created.

Happiness isn't something that is just allowed for a special few. It can absolutely be yours if you want it, you believe you can have it and that you are worthy enough to deserve it.

Over the next few years you may find that your self-belief and self-worth can start to take a bit of a hit.

Situations can happen that can shape your view of yourself, like taking tests and failing, or thinking that others may not like you. Negative comments can easily make you doubt yourself or question your ideas.

Someone telling you you are not good enough or capable enough, can make you believe that you aren't.

If you walk away with one thing from this journey, then it should be with the knowledge that...

The only way you can have true happiness in your life is if you believe in yourself, truly love yourself and know that you are absolutely worthy of creating a wonderful life for yourself.

You deserve to be happy, we all do, and over the next few sections hopefully you will come away with the same belief.

So...are you ready to get happy?

The Science Bit

Just as lots of research and study went into finding out that we have the ability to grow our brain, lots of research and study has gone into the science of happiness and how we can bring more of it into our lives.

Psychologists (Scientists who study the mind and human behaviour) have been looking into happiness for some time and over the next section we will learn about the results of all this research and lots of different ways you can bring more happiness into your own life.

The science behind the study of happiness is called **Positive Psychology.**

Now it is very likely that this is something that you have not heard of before. It may seem complicated and challenging but, don't worry we will get there together.

So, what is Positive Psychology?

In the past Psychologists tended to study the worst things in life; what problems people have. They would study what makes someone sad or depressed. They would study what goes wrong in the world and through that study they would they could find strategies to help people, communities and countries deal with their problems and get better.

Over the past 20 years or so Psychologists have started to look at it from a completely different angle.

Positive Psychology is the scientific study of what makes our lives worth living, what causes people to be happy, what goes right in the world and how we can build on the best of life.

Positive Psychologists are interested in helping people live more positive, fulfilling and happier lives using what they have learned.

It doesn't mean that Positive Psychology ignores what lessons can be learnt from the real problems people face on a daily basis; it is there to work alongside these lessons.

It's there to say "As much can be learnt from strengths and can be from weaknesses" or "As much can be learnt from what goes right in the world as can be from what goes wrong."

In simple terms we can say that traditional Psychology is the science of what makes people happy and Positive Psychology is the science of what makes people happy.

So, we are not ignoring that sad things do happen.

We can lose people we care about, our parents might split up, which causes us distress and sadness. People can be horrible to us and make us feel bad. We might be suffering from lack of confidence, anxiety or feeling that we are not listened too or feeling a bit worthless, we might feel like we don't fit in, or we have had to move away, which has been difficult.

Disappointments/challenges do happen. You might find yourself in one or more of these situations right now. Just trying to be positive about it is not going to make the difficulties go away but looking at how we can create more happiness our lives can help us deal with these situations and find ways of coping, so we can move on a bit more easily.

If you look at the news for instance, you will notice that it is mostly negative stories that are reported such as wars, killings, hunger, poverty or starvation, probably 90% of the stories will be negative with possibly one positive story at the end.

It could make you start to believe that there are more nega-tive/bad things that happen in the world than good...and that is just not true.

You definitely need to work harder to find positively out there. Negative emotions are three times stronger and more powerful than positive emotions so it's not just the case that you can say "I'll be more positive"; you actually have to work at it.

The good news is it is achievable; small changes can make a big difference, it's about making positive daily habits and after twenty one days you will have rewired your brain into a more positive setting (but just like with growth mindset, you need to keep up with your daily habits or you will find your brain will reset itself in no time.)

So, we know it's not just about trying hard to be more posi-tive, because negative thoughts/emotions are stronger, (you need three positive thoughts for every panel out one nega-tive thought/emotion) we actually have to make conscious decisions to reduce the amount of negativity in our lives and replace these negative thoughts, feelings and words with more positive compassionate thoughts and kinder words.

Now hopefully you have already started the process with......**being grateful for what you already have.**

Gratitude is an instant happiness booster (remember we said that being grateful releases a hormone in your brain called serotonin. - (the happiness hormone?)

Practising being grateful every day and allowing it to become a daily habit will, after twenty one days, rewire your brain to start looking for more things to be grateful for and start the process of replacing a negative outlook with a more positive one.

Jar of Gratitude

So, a great activity to make sure you are focusing on all the amazing things you are grateful for is to start a gratitude jar. This activity comes to us from a wonderful lady called Pamela.

Pamela used her jar to collect all the fantastic and happy memories she made and was grateful for, with her family thought the year. At the end of the year she would open her jar and go through all the scraps of paper remembering all the fantastic and special times she had had.

So find a jar with a lid, decorate it how you like and when you are feeling grateful for whatever reason, write what it is you are grateful for on a scrap of paper and place in you jar to keep it safe.

These gratitude's could be anything such as a spending time with someone you love or a lovely gift you received, or something kind that you did for something else that made you feel good about yourself, or something kind that someone did for you.

It's great to be able to look back on at the end of the year like Pamela or it can be very useful to have when you are not feeling very grateful or happy about life. You can dip into your gratitude jar at any point for an instant positive boost when you need it.

So we've looked at gratitude and being more grateful in our lives, but what else can we do in order to bring in more happiness and joy? Well the best place to start is to start with you.

Look at the way you notice the world around you. Are you more focused on the negative times throughout your day or are you letting all the great times you have had, be in your focus? Are you negative about yourself? Do you believe in yourself? Are you kind to yourself?

Looking at yourself and how you view the world and you is really important. Be honest with yourself, do you think you are a positive or a negative person?

Did you know that...

90% of your happiness is **not** determined by what happens externally around you. According to Positive Psychologist Shawn Achor, 90% of your happiness is determined by the way your brain chooses to process all of these external things. And although some of this will be determined by your genetics (the way you were born) 40% of it is completely up to you.

In other words,...You can choose happiness!

Do you remember the word...

Neuroplasticity - the ability of the brain to change through focus, effort and learning?

Well just as we use this to change our brain from a fixed mindset to a growth mindset, we can also use the power of neuroplasticity to change our brain from a negative mindset to a more positive one.

When you are intensely focusing your brain on the positive and bringing in more positivity into your life, you are making strong neurone connections for this positivity.

But most incredibly your brain has an amazing way of weakening the other connections between neurones that aren't being used at that time, so the less negative you are the weaker the connections for negativity become.

That means that you can rewire your brain so you will automatically start to lead a more positive life with less negative thoughts and feelings in it.

Now we did say this will take hard work, focus and effort, (remember negative is stronger than positive.) so lets look first at what we can dump in order to clear the way for positivity.

How do you react to situations that don't go your way?

Getting rid of some negative habits and creating more positive habits will start the process of retraining the brain.

First of all there are a few things you will need to dump in order to do this. Most of what you need to dump will be semi-conscious and will be a reaction that comes quickly.

It will take a bit of work to retrain your brain to not react in these ways when life doesn't go your way, but it will be worth it.

1. You'll need to dump the excuses.

Making excuses; may make you feel better about yourself for not taking action but in the long run, they only stop you doing what you want to do and learn. They stop you growing and they are happiness drainers.

First of all, if you find yourself making lots of excuses, you need to understand why?

Most people make excuses, do it to protect themselves and tend to do it out of fear or self-doubt...

The fear of failing, fear of uncertainty, fear of embarrassment, fear of taking responsibility, fear of being criticised.

The next time you feel an excuse coming on, ask yourself, *"why am I making this excuse?"* and then try not to do it.

2. You'll need to dump the blame game.

Just like excuses, blaming others for what you have or what you don't have, for what you feel and don't feel, to defend your behaviour is not on.

It just allows you to think you are hard done by and nobody lives a happy positive life thinking that.

So the next time you are about to blame someone else, remember that you can choose your happiness and it's up to you that can decide how you are going to deal with the situation.

3. You'll need to quit the criticism.

Criticising others and their choices. Just because something is different or weird to you it doesn't mean that it is not great.

Although we are all different, we all want to be happy, be loved, listened to and feel that we are of value.

Letting go of criticism will free you to open your mind to new and exciting possibilities.

4. You'll need to dump the attitude.

If something doesn't go your way, or you don't get what you want, is there a massive drama, with complaints of "*It's not fair*" "*I never get what I want?*". Do you start to get defensive, aggressive, or rude to others?

Are you constantly moaning about the things, people and situations that make you unhappy?

Do you get told you are over reacting, and that what you are complaining about is not worth the tears, and tantrums?

The next time something doesn't go your way, or you don't get what you want, think to yourself "is this really worth me exploding, complaining, moaning and flying off the handle for?

If this is you, and you struggle to control your reactions, you may find that you just don't fully understand your emotions and how they work yet. That's fine, there is a section that is dedicated to this later on so for now don't sweat it, we'll cover it later.

So, you are grateful and you have dumped the excuses. Next you have to look at how you can replace negative influences (the ones we can control) with positive ones.

This list is just a few of the negative influences you may have in your life right now:

Lack of sleep, lack of self-belief, negative friends, unhealthy foods, worrying, lack of exercise, lack of confidence, too much screen time, negative emotions.

And here are some more positive influences that you might like to bring into your life more:

Music, painting, kindness, hobbies, healthy eating, self-belief, dancing, exercise, hugs, fresh air, creativity, reading, lots of sleep, meditation,, great positive friends, breathing more, laughing.

Reflection

Positive influences would I like to bring more of into my life, are? (They don't need to just be from the list above)

. . .

Negative influences would I like to remove from my life are?

(Again they don't need to just be from the list above)

Think of examples of where you have sabotaged your progress by making an excuse and remember that incident. Bring it to mind whenever you feel like doing it again.

Excuse —

No time for healthy choice.

No energy.

Too stressed —

Need comfort.

Find Joy in the Journy.

*Put of
God*

For me this was big lesson. I was always one for thinking *"I'll be happy when my business is successful."* or *"I'll be happy once we move into a bigger house."* It felt that I was always chasing happiness and it always seemed just out of reach. I'm sure many of you have felt the same.

"Appreciate life even if it's not perfect. Happiness is not the fulfilment of what we wish for, but an appreciation of what we have. The present moment is filled with Joy and Happiness, if you look for it you will see it"

Thich Nhat Hanh
A pretty cool Vietnamese Buddest Monk,
global spiritual leader, poet and peace activist

Have you ever thought...?

"I'll be happy if..."

If you look for it

"I'll be happy if...I pass that test."

"I'll be happy if...that person stops being mean to me."

"I'll be happy if...I get that new game."

The problem with "I'll be happy if..." is that once you pass the test there will always be another test waiting around the corner (which will probably be even harder) and there will always be another new game that will be coming out.

Of course, if that person stops being horrible to you, it probably will make you feel a lot happier, but in life there will always be people out there who will try and make others feel bad for whatever reason (usually because they feel bad about themselves)

So saying "I'll be happy if..." is pointless as you will always be chasing after it.

You need to get happy **now!** We are not here to chase happiness for the rest of our lives. We are here to bring our own happiness right now and there are so many things that you can be happy for right now. Even if it doesn't fell like it (dig deep, we're sure you'll find something that makes you happy)

If you decide you are going to get happy right now, you may be surprised where it will take you...

Richard Branson is one of the most famous business men in the world. He is the owner of Virgin and many other businesses. He is very rich and successful, and this is what he has to say on the subject...

"I know I'm fortunate to live an extraordinary life, and that most people would assume my business success, and the wealth that comes with it, have brought me happiness. But they haven't; in fact, it's the reverse. I am successful, wealthy and connected because I am happy."

What Richard Branson is saying is that he has always made happiness a priority and because he was happy in life he was able to become successful. (He also has a growth mindset and has tried and failed lots of times in business and is still on of the most successful businessmen of all time.)

So happiness has to come first. If we are constantly chasing after something we don't have we are immediately put into a negative discontented state of mind. It also means that we will value our successes based on the material processions we have managed to accrue rather than on our personal growth, how we have challenged ourselves, our personal achievements and by the things that are really important such as our relationships, our friends and our family.

Being successful financially and having lots of possessions will not necessarily mean you will be happy. Especially if you have worked so hard all your life that you have not had time to share your success with anyone. Working hard is a good thing but not if it is at the expense of personal relationships and having balance in your life.

Take some time to think about your future and your future self.

It may seem a long way off but try and visualise your life when you are grown up. What do you want it to look like? What do you see yourself doing?

Is it something that will make you rich or is it something that you feel passionate about?

Are you always working or is your life full of all the things that truly make you happy?

You might not have any idea about what you want to do when you grow up but having an idea of how you want to life your life, how you to feel may help you make future decisions about which path to take.

The happiness advantage

Did you know that your brain in a positive state is actually 31% more productive than in a neutral or negative state?

When you raise your level of positivity you are actually raising your level of ability to learn, your intelligence and your creative skills.

This is what Shawn Achor describes as the **happiness advantage.**

If you walk into school in a positive state of mind you straight away have a 31% advantage on anyone else that has come in a negative or even neutral state. It means that your brain will work even more successfully, faster and more intelligently and that means you are off to a winning start.

Waking up and not wanting to get out of bed because you've not had enough sleep, moaning about having to get dressed, getting straight on a technical device and watching Youtubers or streamer playing action games, not having a good breakfast is **not** going to get your brain into a positive state of mind.

A great morning routine will set you off to a flying start...

Remember the affirmations we talked about at the beginning of the book? try waking up first thing as saying.

"I am awake" "I am alive" "I feel great" "I am confident" "I am ready to learn" "I am ready to have fun" "I am capable of doing great things" "I am ready to have a great day"

See how you feel afterwards.

You may think it's a bit daft, but when you look to many successful people in the world, successful business people, successful scientists, successful musicians, successful sportsmen and women, you find that many of them will do this very thing.

Remember Muhammad Ali said:

"It's the repetition of affirmations that leads to belief, and once that belief becomes a deep conviction, great things begin to happen."

There is no doubt that a great morning routine is a success habit that you might want to seriously look at adopting going forward.

Reflection

What is it I say to myself that "I'll happy if.........?"

All the wonderful things that I already have in my life right now, are?

What does being in a state of positively give me?

Why would a great morning routine help me become more positive?

What can affirmations give me apart from just an instant positivity boost?

What else apart from affirmations can I do in the morning to give me the 31% happiness advantage?

SECTION 3 - WHEN YOU'RE SMILING, THE WHOLE WORLD SMILES WITH YOU

"Every time you smile at someone, it is an action of love, a gift to that person, a beautiful thing"

Mother Teresa
Saint of the Catholic church, known for her dedication in looking after the poor and sick and is only a Nobel Peace Prize winner.

When you're smiling, when you're smiling
The whole world smiles with you
When you're laughing, oh when you're laughing

The sun comes shining through
But when you're crying, you bring on the rain

So stop that sighing, be happy again
Keep on smiling, cause when you're smiling

The whole world smiles with you...

These are the words of a famous song from many years ago and they are a perfect example of why we should smile and the effect it can have on not just only yourself but on others around you.

Smiling puts your brain into a positive state and of course that 31% happiness advantage.

Even if you don't feel positive or particularly happy, the physical act of smiling can trick your brain into thinking that you are intact feeling more positive than you actually are.

Smiling is contagious; when you smile it also makes others smile with you.

It happens because of special neurones in our brain called mirror neurones. This is where our brain is stimulated by an outside force, (such as someone yawning in front of you) and our mirror neurones cause us to reflect the same action, (we have a great big yawn too.)

Well, smiling is one of these forces that affects our mirror neurones, so not only do we have the ability to affect our own happiness but we can affect the happiness of others around us too, just by a simple smile.

Now we don't always feel like smiling and it can seem very odd to just randomly smile at nothing, well here's a little exercise that can actually trick your brain into thinking it's happy by smiling.

It does the job and no one else will think you are strange for having a random grin all over your face.

Take a pen and pop it between your teeth... This action makes your lips turn upwards making your brain think that you are smiling.

A few seconds is all it takes, and you are instantly into a positive state of mind.

Top tip - try doing just before you start lessons to gain that 31% advantage.

Laughing can help you learn

How much do we all love these YouTube video clips of animals doing hilarious things or the "try not to laugh" videos of people falling over or kids trying to jump into paddling pools and falling flat on their face...They 're funny right?

But did you know that watching them can actually help you learn.

Laughing makes you more relaxed. It also releases hormones that, not only have a healing effect but put you brain into that all important positive state which we know that makes us learn faster, harder and more intelligently.

So instead of watching videos of other people playing video games or families testing out the next new toy they've been given to review, why not try and watch some funny videos instead.

Top Tip - Just as your mirror neurones can pick

up on positively they can easily pick up on negative influences too, which is why we have to replace as many negatives influences in our lives with as many positive ones as we can.

Think about a funny thing that has happened to you. It could be with your family or your friends. why was it so funny. Remember how you felt at the time. Does it still make to laugh or smile now?

Reflection

What makes me smile?

What makes me laugh out loud?

What activities make me happy?

Just start laughing for no reason. How does this make you feel? Do you think when you need a boost, just the act of laughing could help?

Recalling happy and funny memories are a great way of helping us feel positive and can be used when we fell anxious or scared about something as a way to bring us back from a negative state to a more positive one.

SECTION 4 - HOW TO MAKE FRIENDS AND INFLUENCE PEOPLE.

"Surround yourself with the dreamers and doers, the believers and thinkers, but most of all, surround yourself with those who see greatness within you, even when you don't see it yourself"

Edmond Lee
Author and Dreamer

Friends

Feeling connected to people is very important to your happiness, having great friends in your life can give you confidence, help you feel loved, worthwhile and of course you can make them feel the same.

Although doing the smiling exercise or watching funny videos on your own will help you feel more positive, nothing compares to the laughter and fun that you can share with others.

Finding your tribe...

Surrounding yourself with likeminded people (people who share the same values as you, the same sense of humour for example) can help you have a sense go belonging that makes to feel safe and happy.

You don't need to share all the same interests, but and understanding of what id really important to you, what you really care about and how you treat each other is what will make somebody more than just a friend but actually part of your tribe.

Your vibe attracts your tribe.

If you have a positive, outgoing personality then you are much more likely to attract positive outgoing friends.

You don't need to have hundreds of friends in your life and its's every unlikely that you will get along with everyone you meet.

We all just need a few special people around us that get who we are. (in fact one really special friend is just about all we actually need to make us happy.)

Always remember that working on your friendships is really important as you grow up, especially when it's time to go off in different directions. It's so worth putting in the effort to keep these special friendships going as the bond that is created is different from any other kind of relationship. Lifelong friends know you inside out and will bring you so much joy, happiness and support throughout your life.

Let you friends know that they are extra special by telling them what is it about them that you love so much. Try making them a thank you for being my friend card to show them that you really value they're friendship. Feeling valued is lovely, we all want to feel valued and valuing our friends by telling them what is so great about them will make them feel like they are really important to you.

Negative influences

Do you have some friends that just moan about everything, all day? Nothing is right, everything is doom and gloom?

How do you think that affects you?

Negative energy effects everyone around it and now you know that it is also as contagious as positivity, so how can you make sure you are not negativity influenced by negative friends.

1. Try to be the positive influence of change.

Smart changes you make can cause a ripple effect and if you are determined to live happier more positive life then you can try and influence others around you to be more positive too.

. . .

2. Get strong.

Working on positive daily habits will make sure your brain is as strong as it can be. Then outside negative influences won't affect you so much.

3. Let go!

If neither of the above is working then possibly finding a way to let go of negative friends that are not up for changing might be the only option.

It is known that the 5 main people you surround yourself with has the biggest impact on you.

At the end of the day you are the only person that can choose how you feel, so if it's not working then maybe it's time for a change...

It doesn't mean that you need to tell them or be mean to them, just spending a bit less time with them will help and make sure you rack up the time you spend with likeminded positive people.

Reflection

What are the most important qualities in a good friend?

How do I feel when I am with my friends?

. . .

Is it important to have lots of friends or am I happy to just have a few really good ones? Why do I believe this?

SECTION 5 - BE KIND

"If you can be anything, be kind"

Ellen DeGeneres
TV host, Comedian, Writer, LGBT rights activist,
animals' rights activist and has a
Gorilla Sanctuary in Rwanda built in her name.

Random Acts of kindness

Did you know that act of doing something kind for someone else actually releases happiness hormones from your brain into your body which makes you feel great?

So, it's a **WIN WIN;** you feel great and the person you have done something kind for feels great too.

Not only that, very time you do something kind for someone else you are using the front part of your brain which is where your compassion is developed, the kinder things you do, the kinder you become as your connections in your brain grow stronger.

So just as you can choose to become happier you can choose to become kinder too.

Being kind to others can give you a sense of fulfilment and when you feel fulfilled you feel happier, calmer, and content.

Some examples of **Acts of Kindness**.

Offer to help your teacher

Pop in and see your grandparents or ask a neighbour if they need help

Find out about your nearest food bank and ask family, friends and neighbours to donate.

Send an encouraging message to someone

If you think someone might have a problem offer to listen.

Gift your favourite book to some

Have a non-judgement day

Raise some money for a good cause.

Ask your school if you can start a RAK (random acts of kindness) programme to encourage others

100 Random Acts of Kindness. Why not set yourself a goal of completing 100 acts of kindness.

SECTION 6 - THE ROAD TO RESILIENCE

"If you can't run then walk, If you can't walk then crawl, but whatever you do you have to keep moving forward"

Dr Martin Luther King Jr.
Famous Campaigner for the rights of
African Americans in the 50-60's.
Gave one of the most famous
speeches ever "I have a dream" and
won a Nobel Peace Prize for his work.

As I said at the very beginning of this book, I believe that every child is incredible and that they are all capable of incredible things.

But I also understand that they are not born with some kind of magical super gene that automatically makes them happy, confident or successful.

There is no point hiding away from the fact that they will all face challenges during their lives.

Building residence in our kids is the best way to ensure they can cope with these challenges head on and the next section covers lots of different ways to help them do this.

The Road to Resilience

We wish that life was easy and happy all the time but sadly it's just not the case.

You will have times in your life when are things challenging. Someone might be being mean to you, you may have lost someone close to you, your parents might have split up or may be getting divorced, you may have important exams that are stressing you out, you may be scared of trying something new, you may be having a hard time at school, you may not feel good enough, your best friend might be leaving or you might be moving away.

All these situations can leave us feeling anxious, sad, angry, frustrated, embarrassed, lonely, scared, overwhelmed, on our own, or a little bit lost.

This is all perfectly normal, but what we don't want to happen is, for these periods in our lives to break us completely or for them to end up effecting us for the rest of our lives.

Luckily there is something that you can build within yourself to help you manage these difficult situations and move forward from them in a stronger more positive way. It's called...

RESILIENCE

Resilience is the thing which will make you stronger, braver, feel super confident, and empowered. But what actually is Resilience and why is it important to become a strong resilient person?

Resilience can be described as:

- Your ability to cope with challenges in your life.
- Your ability deal with adversity.
- Your ability to "bounce back" after a setback.

Resilience is not something to are just born with, but it is something that you can build. In order to do that you firstly have to understand why we react to situations in the way we do.

Everyone is different, and everyone reacts differently to different situations. You might find that you fall apart over something that others find a really small insignificant thing, but then you manage to cope really well with a situation that others might find really difficult to deal with.

Within this next section, "The Road to Resilience", we will look at many different areas that will not only help you understand yourself better but we will also give you strategies that you can use in order to build your own resilience.

SUBSECTION A - EMOTIONS AND FEELINGS

"Emotions are much like waves, we can't stop them from coming, but we can choose which one to surf"

Jon Kabat-Zinn
Master of Mindfulness

How to be the boss of your brain

Can you remember when you were a little kid and you would get bursts of anger that felt completely uncontrollable, you would lose the plot and not really understand what was going on? You may still feel like this happens when you don't get your own way, or you feel hard done to in some way.

Your parents may have not understood what was going on and get angry with you, or think you were overreacting, just being badly behaved or tell you to just calm down or go to your room.

But the feelings you were having would be overwhelming and you just wanted someone to listen to you, and help you understand what you were feeling.

The thing is what you were experiencing is absolutely normal and part of the process you have to go through in order to understand your own emotions and how they affect you.

When you are very young, your brain is not developed enough to handle these feelings but each outburst is a learning process that you have to go through until your brain is developed enough to handle things better.

Understanding your emotions is really important. Knowing why we feel the way we feel and remembering that our thoughts and emotions are controlled by our brain is the most important bit.

If you understand that your thoughts and emotions are controlled by your brain, then you can train (rewire) it to handle these emotions and feelings in a more controlled, positive way which will in turn build your resilience allowing you handle difficult situations that cause you stress etc.

We don't just experience strong emotions when we are very young. Strong emotions and feelings are things that you are going to have all through your life. We now know that our brains are continually developing and changing and as such so are our emotions and behaviour.

It's important to understand that it is ok to feel scared, anxious, sad, angry and frustrated but it's when we let ourselves become overwhelmed by these emotions and are unable to move on from them that they can become a problem.

What emotions and feelings do to us physically

Feelings such as anger, sadness (grief), stress, anxiety, send signals to your brain and this then releases hormones (chemicals), **adrenaline** and **cortisol** (also known as the stress hormone) into your system that cause a physical reaction. Feelings of joy and happiness do the same, releasing adrenaline as well as different hormones such as **dopamine** and **serotonin** (also known as the happiness hormone)

When these stress hormones flood your body, they cause your heart to beat faster, creating an overwhelming feeling in your body that is sometimes difficult to cope with and can be scary.

Feeling physically sick, lightheaded, dizzy, shaky can all be the result of these hormones in our body. It is not in your imagination that you are physically feeling this way; the hormones in your system are designed to create a physical reaction to your thoughts and feelings.

For example: You have to do something that makes you feel

nervous, e.g. stand up and do a presentation in front of the class.

When it is your turn your body is flooded with these chemicals and now you feel physically sick. Your body is telling you that you are really ill rather than just a bit nervous at the thought of standing up in front of the class. There is no way you can do your presentation now because you are ill.

Have you ever felt like this in a similar situation, when the physical reaction you are having has taken over and it stops you in your tracks?

Have you ever thought "I'm not stressed out, I'm really sick" in reaction to someone saying "I think you're a bit stressed"? Well you may be interested to know that this reaction is there for a reason and a very good one at that.

It's actually a survival mechanism created to make you aware of danger and understand the difference between something that is safe and good and something that is dangerous and can harm you.

Your feelings and emotions and the physical effects that they have are there in order for you to survive!

So, if you ever need validation that what you are feeling is real and powerful then this is it. The very survival of the human race depended on us feeling these emotions and having these physical reactions.

A long time ago your ancestors lived in a world that was very different to the way we live now. Firstly, they had to hunt for their food and they relied on their emotions to keep themselves alive.

Nowadays lots of things are different. It is very unusual for the people that look after you to put you directly into life threatening situations. You will not be expected to go out and kill a buffalo for your tea with lions surrounding you, trying to hunt that same buffalo to feed to their cubs.

It is more likely that fear/anxiety and the physical feeling you have may just stop you from jumping off a high wall or will make you more cautious about crossing a busy road for the fear of being run over.

The easiest way to understand all of this is to understand that the brain is made up of many parts and each part has a different function.

The old brain (or instinctive brain) is what our ancestors had and it was the Amygdala (A-mig-dula) within this part of the brain that was designed to control the most basic functions in life such as breathing, heart rate, movement, and basic memory. Built for survival it processed behaviour and emotions, and very quick decisions were made based on the feeling of fear, anxiety etc.

Here Psychologist Karen Young describes how it works...

"The amygdala is very small but very powerful part of your brain that is there to warn us of danger and prepare us to respond. The amygdala takes its job VERY seriously. It's like your own fierce warrior, there to protect you, but

sometimes it can take it can work a little too hard, scanning the environment constantly, and warning you of danger when there's really nothing at all to worry about.

Humiliation, embarrassment, being separated from someone you love, missing out on something important, having things not turn out as planned, making mistakes – these all count as potential threats to an amygdala that is fiercely dedicated to keeping you safe and sound. If thoughts are coming from big feelings, sadness or anger, it's also likely that the amygdala is involved."

Over thousands of years we have developed further brain layers around the old brain. This is known as the Frontal Cortex and is where our critical thinking, learning, memory, judgement, language and senses (language, hearing, touch) are processed.

Tapping into the newer part our our brain can help us bring some logic to why we are feeling the way we are.

Just to add to the confusion you will face as you grow up, it's good to know that your Amygdala will reach full adult size before the Frontal Cortex in your brain will. This means that for a period of time you will have an adult size instinctive/reactive part of your brain but you will still only be able to deal logically with your reactions it causes in a child like manner.

It is a tricky time and can be confusing. Talking to someone about how you feel can really help.

Learning and understanding how **you** deal with your own emotions and feelings is the first step in building your resilience and will help you get through the confusing and challenging period you will face as you grow.

This is called your "**Emotional Intelligence**" and the better you understand your own self, the easier it will be to deal with the feelings that you have.

Facing up to the challenges ahead and dealing with difficult times will allow your brain to learn from each experience you go through and help you deal with the next challenge you face.

Let's look at some of the stronger emotions that you will face and hopefully if you are dealing with any of these feelings right now using the strategies provided will help you deal with how you are feeling.

Feeling anxious can be horrible. It is the emotion that makes us feel sick, or gives us a headache. There are many reasons that you may feel stressed or worried: you may have important exams that are stressing you out, you may be scared of trying something new, you may be having a hard time at school, you may not feel good enough, maybe something bad happened to you and although you are ok, you just can't stop thinking that something else is going to go wrong.

Sadness also has a physical effect. You may feel a lump in

your throat, an aching feeling in your chest, pain behind your eyes. You may feel like you want to be alone, curl up in a ball and hide from the world.

Again, there are many reasons that you may feel sad. You've been disappointed, rejected or ignored, you haven't achieved your goals, your best friend might be leaving or you might be moving away, perhaps even something more difficult like, your parents might have split up or may be getting divorced, or someone close to you has died.

Remember feeling a bit of stress or anxiety, sadness, anger is a perfectly normal part of everyday life and these emotions are there for a reason.

A little amount of stress and sadness is actually good for you as it can motivate you to do things an it can provide you with focus to get things done.

Feeling sad shows that you care and that you have empathy for others. It also signals to others that you might need some support, kindness and care. It can also be signal to you of something you want to change. If you are unhappy with a situation it may be time to change it.

Adopting a positive attitude towards these emotions (i.e. seeing negative emotions as a good thing) will help build your self-belief giving you the power to handle your feelings and difficult situations. ("if I can handle this, I can handle the next difficult thing.") This in turn builds your resilience, which in turn gives you the confidence to go for new exciting challenges in life.

If you think about it, if you just feel happy all the time why would you be motivated to try new things, take risks, challenge yourself or push yourself to achieve? Negative emotions are much more likely to do that, so it's not that we want to get rid of negative emotions and never experience them, it's that we don't want them to overwhelm us, completely take over or become unmanageable.

Just don't try and avoid your feelings, thinking that we have to be positive all the time. Just brushing them aside won't work no matter how hard you try.

Embrace your emotions

The only way to deal with situations that worry you, scare you or make you feel sad is to face them head on.

Remember the word **fear** can stand for two things:

Forget Everything And Run or Face Everything And Rise

Often when you are feeling really scared, anxious, sad, hurt, embarrassed about things, the people closest to you (because they actually want to show you that they love and care for you) will tell you that everything is fine and that's it's all ok or they just take away the thing that is making you feel this way, because it's hard to see you scared, or upset.

Even though it is out of love, just telling you things are ok when you feel that they are not or taking away what is making you feel this way is not going to help.

In fact, it can actually make you feel even worse. You know

inside something isn't right so telling you that everything is fine will just make you feel that you are on your own and teaching you to completely avoid dealing with the feelings you are having at the time is even worse.

Avoiding dealing with your feelings is extremely unhealthy. It might make you feel better or safe in the short term but in the long-term learning to feel safe by avoiding how you feel, will lead you to a place where you emotionally shut down, you won't be able to cope with difficult situations and your mental health could really suffer.

Running away and hiding your feelings will not make these feelings go away. In fact they will only get worse and the last thing you want is to happen is for the worry monster to take over.

If you let the worry monster take over, you may find yourself constantly feeling anxious or stressing out or sad about things that haven't even happened yet. This is when your emotions are out of control and stopping you from living a happy life.

Worrying, being anxious, sad, scared and all the physical feelings that come with it, if bottled up and kept to yourself, can sometimes present itself in different ways.

You may find yourself getting really angry because you don't understand how you really feel, and when you are angry your behaviour can sometimes deteriorate, you can be rude or aggressive, you might find that you melt down over what may seem to others like a really small thing. This behaviour can lead others to think you are overreacting or just behaving badly and then in turn you can think that they don't understand, care or you are not being listened too.

Often the actual problem you are facing is hidden in this behaviour and it's not that easy for others to understand.

Just like the small child who would lose the plot when given the red cup when they wanted the blue one, if we are confused about what we are feeling then often our behaviour becomes confusing too.

Being a worry monster can also cause you to become extremely sensitive to what is happening around you and little things can become much bigger than they actually are.

Remember that the connections in your brain become stronger and stronger as you learn new behaviour so each time you break through a fear, the brain remembers that and the next time you face your fears the easier it will be.

Becoming the boss of your brain and being able to tell the amygdala "alright pal, I've got this" will take work as the amygdala is pretty overprotective, but there are many short term strategies you can use to help you push through these negative feelings and emotions and feel calmer in the moment. There are also some longer term strategies to help you deal with the underlying issues going forward.

So embrace all your emotions and feelings and allow yourself the time to understand why you are feeling a certain way.

If you are feeling sad, let yourself feel sad, if you are feeling angry that's fine, it's ok and perfectly normal. If you are scared that's ok too. Knowing and understanding why you feel a certain way is good, but only if you can also find a way work through these feelings.

Being aware of your thoughts and feelings is so important. Understanding them, and also how you react to them, will help you move forward.

Finding strategies that can help you from melting down immediately every time you don't get what you want, or flying off the handle straightaway when you feel angry, will allow you to grow your emotional intelligence going forward and build your strength and resilience.

And don't forget, happiness is an emotion too.

Because we don't feel bad or ill when we are happy it's probably the one emotion that we don't really take the time to fully recognise (remember negative is stronger than positive). It's difficult to ignore the physical feelings of stress, anger, or sadness so taking the time to acknowledge when you feel happy is as important as acknowledging all the other emotions too.

We will look at how you can really take the time to acknowledge your feelings later, in the last section (Mind, Body & Soul) but for now here's some short- and long-term strategies that can help you get to grips with how you are feeling.

Short term/immediate strategies.

The best way to understand these strategies is when you are feeling calm and safe. There is no point just running to your book to learn them when you are in the middle of feeling stressed or anxious as your brain in that moment will be in full on protection mode and not really able to take the information in.

If you have ever suffered from anxiety, stress, sadness, anger, fear then these will help. If you haven't they are still great to learn for the future.

Just Breathe

Breathing when you are feeling panicky, stressed out and anxious is not always easy. Your chest might feel tight and breathing in can feel like you can't catch a breath, and this can make you feel worse. Trying to breathe in can sometimes feel impossible, so don't ... just breathe **out**.

The aim is to be able to get a breath and get your breathing under control, then to be able to slow your breathing down enough so you can feel calm.

Breathe out as fast and hard as you can. If you only take a short breath back in that is fine, just breathe out again and again until you feel like the breaths coming back in are a bit bigger. Then breathe out again only this time slower, still a big breath out but slow it down. Then a slow breath in and a slow breath out. At this point close your eyes and just concentrate on the breath, slowly in and out.

Your body is designed to breathe in automatically after you breathe out so always breathe out first when trying to calm yourself down.

Anchoring (How to be in a safe and happy place at anytime)

There once was a girl called Abigail who was overcome with fear and anxiety on a regular basis. The feelings would overwhelm her and stop her from doing things that she really wanted to do. Luckily for Abigail she had a special lady in her life, who taught Abigail how to anchor.

When you are not feeling stressed or anxious, find yourself a quiet space, sit down, close your eyes and take a few deep breaths. In and out, clear your head and think of your breathing, slowly in and out.

Think of a memory of a time when you were in a really positive and safe space. A really happy place where you felt happy, safe, loved and secure. Visualise this place in your mind, hold that memory in your head, think about how you felt at that time, what you were doing, who were you with, what it sounded like, what it felt like.

Don't let the visualisation of your special place disappear. Keep it in your mind and as you are thinking of this place and feeling relaxed and secure, take your thumbs and second fingers on your hands and press them together. Keep thinking of your happy place and keep pressing your fingers and thumbs together. Anchor that thought into your fingers, over and over again.

Keep doing it until you feel secure that every time your thumbs and fingers touch you will be able to be right back in that safe happy place.

You may need to practise this a few times until you have really anchored your thoughts into your fingers.

Now if you find yourself in a place where you feel anxious you will be able to touch your fingers and immediately you will be able to take a breath, close your eyes and be right back in your safe and happy place, breathe the anxiety away and feel calm and secure.

The Worry Balloon

Get a balloon of your favourite colour. Before you blow it up, get a piece of paper and write a list of all the things that are worrying you. Once you have written your list, tear it up into tiny pieces stick the pieces into the balloon and blow it up. Take the balloon side and let it go. Watch all your worries fly away into the sky. Take some deep breaths as you watch them go.

The Chill Out Jar

Create your own calming and soothing jar just using an empty jar with a lid, some warm water, glitter glue and some extra glitter. Fill the jar half full with the warm water and add the glue and glitter. Every time you feel a bit stressed out then shake the jar and watch as the glitter starts to float around to the bottom. As you are watching remember to breathe.

A letter of Love

Often when we feel sad it because we miss someone. Maybe a relative or a pet has died, or your best friend moved away. This sadness is because we loved and cared about that person and we miss them in our lives.

Writing a letter of love can often help as it gets your feelings out of your head and into words. Tell them how you felt about them, what was it about them that was so special, recall any happy times you shared together.

Making the letter something special and positive will help you remember the good times together. Of course, the other person won't receive the letter, but you can keep it and in a safe place and look back on it from time to time when you feel sad.

Hopefully over time your feelings will move on from just sadness to some happiness that you has such a special bond with that person and the times you shared together were happy special times.

Journaling

Just like with the letter idea, journaling can help get your feelings out. If they are anxious feelings, sad, angry or frustrated feelings, getting them into writing can help you start to process how you are feeling.

Remember these emotions you are feeling are normal and it is important that you respect how you are feeling and don't try and pretend everything is ok.

. . .

Have a good cry if it's what you feel like doing. Get these feelings out and don't bottle them up.

Dance

Dancing and music are a great way to help you feel better when you are stressed out. Shaking off the excess hormones that are in your body is a great release and dancing to your favourite music can lift your spirits.

If you are nervous about a situation, put on some music that makes you feel powerful and strong and jump around a bit. You might feel quite different about what is making you nervous.

The Worry Box

If you find that you worry a lot, and you can't stop having thoughts that make you worried throughout the day, then a worry box can help. You may be asking a parent lots of questions about things that make you worried all the time.

Make a decision that you are only going to give a certain amount of time to these thoughts every day and ask a parent or a trusted person if they would be happy to sit with you at a certain time each day and go through the things that are worrying you.

If you have worrying thought, write it down and put it in

the box. Try not to give any more time to thinking about it as once it is in the box, you know it will be looked at later.

Hopefully by the time you come to go though your worries some of them won't feel as big as they did when you first thought them. You may even find that at the beginning you have lots of worries in your box and then over time the amount gets smaller and smaller.

When we bottle our worries up they get bigger and bigger and when we get them out they often get smaller and smaller. Don't forget once you have gone over what is worrying you throw the bits of paper away.

Reflection

What part of my brain is responsible for detecting threats?

When I don't get what you want or are told I can't do something how do I react in the moment?

How would I like to react in these situations?

Do I feel that I am in control of my emotions or do they sometimes get the better of me?

How do I feel right now?

. . .

Do I think of myself as a bit of a worrier or a am I pretty chilled with life?

I think am a bit of a worrier. What is it that worries me and what do I think I can do to work through my worries?

I am chilled out. What is it that that makes me feel this way?

When I feel sad my body feels like?

When I feel anxious my body feels like?

The next time I feel my mind and body over reacting I am going to try and......?

The in Laws
Ego free

SUBSECTION B - IT'S GOOD TO TALK.

"Sometimes you just need to talk about something, not necessarily to get sympathy or help, but just to kill it's power by allowing the truth of things to hit the air"

Karen Salmansohn
Best-selling author
has sold over a million books.

If you find yourself in a situation that is making you feel stressed, worried, angry or sad never ever bottle it up and keep it to yourself.

Short term strategies are great but actually you may need something long term to help process all your thoughts and feelings and talking is the best long-term strategy there is.

Sharing how you are feeling is the most important thing you can do. There are lots of other people out there that you can share your worries with, for instance your parents, a good friend, a teacher, or head teacher, your coach or leader of your sports club or scout/ cubs / brownie leader or youth worker.

Often talking to someone outside the situation is easier as you will be able to talk freely about how you are feeling without worrying that you may upset anyone or worrying that they have own opinions on what is happening and don't understand your point of view.

So if you find at first that you would prefer to talk to someone who is not your parent or directly responsible for looking after you and that is fine.

If you just don't know of anyone that you feel you can open up to don't worry as there are many organisations that you can get in touch with who have already helped thousands of children deal with thousands of different problems and issues and will always have someone there ready to listen.

(Details of organisations that can help are at the back of your journal.)

Remember there is always a solution to every problem. Nothing is so big that is can't be resolved and a **"problem shared is definitely a problem halved."**

Why is it so important to talk?

Building up the courage to talk to someone might feel hard. You may be worried that you won't be taken seriously but finding someone you trust and sharing how you are feeling can help in so many ways.

Don't ever feel weak that you have asked for help with a problem. Plucking up the courage to share your feelings is one of the bravest things you can do and although it may seem scary, once you have spoken to someone they will be able to help you process what is going on and what it is you are feeling, and once you know what it is you are dealing with you can start the process of feeling better.

Saying things out loud, even if you are not sure they make sense or not, makes them less scary, whereas bottling up these feelings can make them not only seem bigger than they actually are but also very confusing.

Sharing your thoughts can also get rid of the horrible physical feeling you have been experiencing (remember when stressed or facing fear you brain releases hormones throughout your body that can make you feel physically sick). Many people describe it as a feeling like a weight has been lifted off their chest. Your body relaxes, and you feel lighter. Once you are physically feeling better it is easier to work through the mental feelings.   Shoulders drop.

When you talk to someone, they might see what is happening from a different perspective and they could help you see it from a new perspective too. They will be able to reassure you that what you are feeling is perfectly normal, you are not alone and that you will get through it.

If you can find a way to get really good at being open and honest about your feelings now, then challenges and stressful situations that you face as you go through the rest of your life will become easier to deal with.

Writing your thoughts and feeling down first may help you process what you want to talk about.

Get busy doing the things you love

Once you have started the process of understanding of how you feel, have shared your problems and feel more confident in dealing with all these emotions and feelings then filling your life doing things that you love can be a great distraction and can help you not focus on these difficult feelings all the time.

So get things off your chest, then go and dance, play, have a game of football with your friends, make something, do something nice for someone else, paint, draw, run around, spend time with people that make you happy, watch a great film, read a book, set some goals or write a list of all the things you love to do and tick them off.

Just never sit alone in your thoughts for too long and never let a problem grow into a monster. When you do then you are most likely to become angry and frustrated and that's when your behaviour can deteriorate. Lashing out at others will never solve that is going on inside you. Always know that there is someone out there that will listen and understand.

Reflection

The person I would most trust to share my problems with is?

What would worry me the most about talking through my problems with someone else?

If I could share some worries now what would they be?

How do I feel now I have written them down?

I have already talked to someone about a problem, how do I feel?

I have already talked to someone about a problem and I feel they weren't the right person and I am still not feeling better; what do I think I should do?

Listen to what your instincts are telling you. If you think you need some help or advice then talk to someone, get over the fear and get the help you need...

SUBSECTION C - STAYING TRUE TO WHO YOU ARE

" I can't tell you the key to success,

but the key to failure, is trying to please everyone"

Ed Sheeran
Only one of the greatest
musicians of our generation

Be You, Stay True

When we are younger it feels like one of the most important things to do is to fit in. Everybody wants to feel liked, and if we feel we are a bit different from others it is sometimes easier to change who we are in order to fit in with everyone else.

This is actually a huge mistake and the older you get you start to understand that being a bit different can be a great thing. Standing out from the crowd and being an individual can open up doors to you when you are older especially when you could be up against lots of others, for instance when applying for the same job, or making a pitch to a company with your business idea.

Often many very successful or famous people started out in life feeling very different from others around them, but by becoming strong in their self-belief, staying true to how they are, being unique and individual and following their own path has given them the opportunities that just wouldn't have been available to them if they had tried to fit in or had followed the crowd.

In order to be able to do this you have to get strong, you have to build your self-belief and confidence, get resilient and not let others' opinions about you effect the decisions you make.

Be yourself. Embrace your quirks. Being weird is a wonderful thing.... I have a football team now, that's pretty cool!"

Ed Sheeran

Bullying

We understand that at times it can feel very challenging, to stay true to who you are, especially if others are being mean to you.

But you can decide whether or not you will allow it to affect your own self-worth and you own opinion of yourself for the rest of your life, or if you are willing to put in the effort to work on yourself, your self-belief and confidence to overcome these kinds of challenges.

It does sound like hard work, and it is understandable that you would feel hurt, upset and confused about why others would want to make you feel this way. Trying to think about what must be going on inside their head in order for the to make you fell like that might help.

Do you think a bully has a fixed mindset or a growth mindset?

Many people who bully others do so because they don't feel great about who they are (they might be having a terrible time themselves) and it actually gives them an instant boost (hormones are released in their brain) when they are mean to others.

In that moment they feel better about themselves. The feeling doesn't last long, and they have to keep doing it to get that hit of feeling better.

Bullies don't even tend to think about how they are affecting the person they are being mean to and that is why you must try and get really strong within yourself, if this is happening to you.

The truth is hurt people...hurt people. (In other words, if someone is hurting inside, they are likely to hurt others.)

What is really sad is, we can get the same instant boost and release of the same hormones in our brain by doing something nice for someone else instead.

Being kind gives us the same feeling as being mean.

The big different is, that the feeling we get from being kind to others lasts a whole lot longer than the felling we get from being mean. We are also left with a good feeling about who we are, whereas being mean leaves us feeling pretty rubbish about who we are.

Always remember that people have the ability to change the way they are treating you (or someone you know). It is most likely to be because of their own low self-esteem (lack of confidence or self-worth) and they are doing these things because of their own thoughts and feelings. It's not because they are a bad person and it doesn't mean that they will always be like this.

Just in the same way that you aren't either an all good or bad person and your thoughts and feelings will change all the time too.

If you really think about it, I'm sure you could think of a time when you have maybe been mean to someone and then have changed the way you have been to that person,

Next, think of a time when someone has been mean to you and are now completely different to you. None of us are perfect and you will probably find that the time when you were mean to someone was a time when you didn't feel that great about yourself.

Changing your behaviour to become a better person is a good thing but changing who you are because you want to fit in or others want you to be more like them is completely different.

As you grow up and especially as you begin your teenage years, you may find this is one of the biggest challenges that you have face.

Learning about yourself and who you are, will help you understand what is important to you.

What are your beliefs, what are your hopes and dreams, what are your strengths, your weaknesses, what are you passionate about, what makes you happy, what makes you sad?

Being true to yourself is that inner voice inside you telling you if you are on the path you want to be on or if you are changing direction. It is standing up for what you believe in and being confident that your are good enough and your decisions are good enough.

Knowing that you are in charge, you have the power, you are the boss of you and you set your own rules. Being true to yourself will also help you be true to others, kinder, more understanding, compassionate and willing to help when others are in need.

Knowing what you believe to be right will make you stronger, allow you to walk away from situations you are uncomfortable with and stand up for what you believe in.

It's really worth while taking the time to truly understand

who you are, and make choices about how you want to live, knowing that you are in control of those choices.

You may at this stage in your life not feel like you are always in control of the choices you make, and that may be true in terms of things you are allowed to do but you are definitely in control of being the kind of person you want to be.

CULTURE OF COMPARISON

There's no doubt you are living in a challenging world, with the rise of reality TV, and social media. With apps like Instagram and Snapchat it is easy to start thinking that everyone out there is leading an amazing life. Everyone looks amazing, is doing amazing jobs and is happy all the time.

You might feel that your life just doesn't live up to this and you can start to believe you and your life are not good enough.

The truth is reality TV and Instagram are NOT real. People only ever post pictures of their best self and often have their hair and make-up done for them by professionals. Reality TV is the same and it really should really be called FAKE TV. Everything is set up, so you believe that this is what a great life looks like and in reality, it is not like that at all.

It is giving you a false impression of what the world is like and it is leading a lot of people to believe that they're own life is worthless, or that the only way to have a great life is to become famous, look like a reality TV star or be a Youtuber/Streamer and make millions.

These people have sadly become our role models in life. In the past great sportsmen and women were our role models, people who had achieved great things like astronauts, scientists, musicians or actors.

Having role models that are just based on how they look is so damaging to your own self-esteem and we are already starting to see the damage it is doing, especially to young women (although there is a lot of evidence that young men are affected too)

The constant comparison to others every day, happiness being dependent on how many likes they get on Facebook or Instagram, the pressure to be popular and look a certain way is causing a lot of young women and some men to suffer from a number of mental health issues, such as depression, major anxiety and even things like anorexia.

The truth is it does not make you a better person if you have false lips, a tiny waist and a huge behind. You are worth so much more than what you just look like and what we want to do is to empower you to feel great about who you are and what you are.

If you feel empowered then you can take on the world, and possibly even change it, and a great way to start is to be kind to others and to yourself.

The other danger with social media is that you are not even comparing like for like. Steven Furtick describes...

"the reason we struggle with insecurity is because we compare our behind-the-scenes with everyone else's highlight reel"

In other words, we look at our own lives and compare them with the bits that others choose us to see; the very best bits of their lives, the best bits that they have selected.

It's not very often that people share the worst parts of their day or how they are really feeling and a picture of them looking absolutely terrible to go with it.

A really good example of this comes from an incredible young woman called Siobhan Dobie who has created a website of blogs sharing her journey through crippling anxiety and depression.

You can find Siobhan at acutecrisis.com.

In her blog post **" Instagram V's Reality: The truth behind the pictures"** she shares a series of pictures that she had posted on Instagram .

She writes

"After I shared my website with friends and family, a family friend told me that she was surprised to hear I had been suffering, as on social media I appeared to be doing fine. That really made me think; you only share the high-lights of your life and this could be due to a

variety of reasons. A lot of people feel pressured to have the perfect life documented on social media, but personally I don't like sharing my low moments, as it makes others uncomfortable and I can feel embarrassed. In this day and age, seeing others living seemingly flawless lives can make us feel insecure and inferior, however, you must keep in mind that not everything is as it appears. To prove how deceitful social media can be I'm sharing a few pictures from my personal Instagram."

She then goes on to share exactly how she was really feeling when each of the photo's were taken.

In one picture taken on Christmas day, she looks happy, and like she is having a great time, but in truth she hadn't been able to get out of bed the previous four days...

"I thought I would have to spend Christmas Day in bed but I did well. This was the first day in maybe weeks, that I got properly dressed and wore make up. Had it been any other day I would've stayed in pyjamas and moped, but since it was Christmas, I made an effort for my family. From scrolling past this picture, you would think I was having a lovely Christmas break but in truth it was a battle to make it through the day."

Siobhan's blog shows just how different a person's life can be like compared to what you see. So although Social

Media can be great in many ways, don't be fooled into believing that everything you are looking at is always the true story.

A huge thank you to Siobhan for allowing us to share her blog with you. Sharing her story takes courage, especially when she is facing such difficult challenges of her own. She wants to help others in the same situation, which is an incredible, brave thing to do and we feel she an amazing role model to other young people throughout the world.

YOU ARE WHAT YOU SAY YOU ARE.

" Be impeccable with your word. Speak with integrity, say only what you mean. Avoid using the word to speak against yourself or to gossip about others. Use the power of your word in the direction of truth and love"

Don Miguel Ruiz

Another way of saying **"you are what you say you are"** is **"whatever you say about yourself is true"**.

So if you say things about yourself like **"I am a really good person and I take care of others"** then that is true, but if you say **"I'm rubbish, I'm not good at anything"** and **"I'm not a good friend"** then that is also true to you.

At the end of the day you are what you believe you are

(what you believe is your reality) so working on your self-belief will help you become the person you want to be.

Getting rid of negative thoughts about yourself is a must!

Your thoughts about yourself can be described as **self-talk** and **negative self-talk** (negative thoughts about yourself) will only make you feel unhappy.

Getting rid of negative self-talk

We all do it, we can be really nasty to ourselves at times.

Now if you have done something that wasn't great then regretting doing it is good, but feeling like you are a bad person and not worthy go love and friendship is self-destructive and unhelpful.

No one is perfect, we all make mistakes, we all do things we wished we hadn't, but don't ever feel like you are not good enough because that will never be the truth.

Everyone is unique, special and different in their own way. That's what's so great about the world. Oh how dull it would be if we were all the same.

I'm sure we all agree that being a bully is not good, so why do so many of us bully ourselves saying things like,

"I'm not pretty enough" "I'm not smart enough" "I'm too fat" "I'm too thin" 'I'm really boring" 'I'm not funny enough" ?

This kind of negative self talk is very easy to do, especially living in the world where as we said, comparison to others, through social media etc is an everyday thing.

Make it a priority to get rid of negative self talk and make the decision to be kind to yourself. Life is really precious and so are you. Being kind to others and being kind to yourself is of equal importance.

Using your affirmations daily is a great way to start talking to yourself, about yourself in a positive way.

Use this time to really think what it is about yourself that is great and celebrate that every single day.

'I am freaking awesome!' is a good place to start.

Remember you need three positive thoughts to overcome one negative thought, so you will need three positive affirmations for every negative thought about yourself that you have. So how about...

"I am loved" I am valued" I am a beautiful person, inside and out" " I care about myself and others" "I am special and unique" "I deserve to be happy" "I will lead my own path" "I will stay true to who I am because who I am is good enough" "I am not judgmental of myself or others" "I am important" "I am worthy of wonderful things".

When you have a negative thought, look for things around that thought that you can turn into a positive.

We know that you are going to face challenges in your life.

Not everyone in your world is going to be kind to you, not everyone in your world is even going to like you.

If you can get your head around this now and make sure that you continue to work on yourself, become confident with who you are, be kind to yourself, and stay true to who you are, even in adversity, you will lead a happier life, where challenges and adversity may bend you a little but they won't break you.

When the wind blows really hard, a tree doesn't just let it break it, it grows stronger roots to steady itself and that's all you need to do too.

WHAT OTHERS THINK OF YOU IS NONE OF YOUR BUSINESS.

"My Philosophy in life is: It's none of my damn business what other people say of me and think of me. I am what I am, I do what I do. I expect nothing and accept everything. And it makes life so much easier"

Sir Anthony Hopkins
One of the greatest actors of our time,
he has won on
Oscar and been given a Knighthood.

If I could hand you one gift right now it would be for you to live a life where you didn't care too much about what other people think of you.

The only thing that truly matters is what you really think of yourself.

Sadly the need to be accepted and the fear that we won't be

accepted can be really powerful, overwhelming, and all consuming.

I said earlier about how it is important it is to feel connected to other people and how having great friends can give you a sense of belonging, that makes you feel safe and happy.

Having good connections to others and being happy are intertwined. A sense of belonging is a really important human instinct and while we must embrace that, if you rely on others to make you happy and build your confidence all the time, it can lead to you becoming sensitive, needy and insecure and that doesn't lead to healthy and happy relationships.

Trying to please everyone in order to make you liked is also a sure fire way of leading to disaster. Often trying to please everyone means that you end up pleasing no-one, especially not yourself.

Just trying to be a good person, who is kind and considerate to others, takes others feelings into consideration and genuinely cares is enough. **You are enough!!!**

Now just like any emotion or feeling, the feeling of embarrassment or shame when we don't live up to our own standards or something happens and we make a fool of ourselves, can actually be good for us, as it reminds us that we want to be better. We are more likely to correct and learn from past mistakes if we feel embarrassed about them.

But once again it is when we let these feelings overwhelm

us that they can turn into something unhelpful, like constantly needing people's reassurance or actually changing who you are in order to feel like you fit in.

When you allow yourself to feel judged by others it can cloud your own judgement of what is important to you.

The next time you have a decision to make ask yourself

"what would I do in this situation, if I wasn't worried about other peoples opinions or judgements"

Now this is doesn't mean that we shouldn't care about feedback or criticism. Being able to accept negative feedback and criticism, take it on the chin and learn from it, without it feeling that you are no good or worthless, can help you become a better person.

There will be certain people whose opinion matters more to you than others. That's a good thing; seeking advice or taking on criticism from someone who you respect and trust will only benefit you and help you grow.

But spending all your time focused on what other people think of you, especially people that you don't think too highly of in the first place, will only create self doubt, kill your confidence and affect your self esteem.

Have you ever thought about the fact that, if everyone else is busy worrying about what other people are thinking of them, then they can't be spending too much time actually thinking about you anyway?

Studies show that we believe we would be judged much more harshly for an embarrassing mistake than we actually would be in real life. It's our own internal anxiety about what others think that is the biggest problem.

So let go of that anxiety and start living your life as your true self. Go out and enjoy the things you enjoy, don't worry about making a mistake or you will never take a risk, be spontaneous, have fun, go crazy, and don't let anyone stop you from leading the life that your truly want to lead.

At the end of the day we're sure you'd rather be a **Warrior** than a **Worrier** and **Fierce** rather than **Fearful**.

" Create the highest grandest vision possible for your life.

Because you become what you believe"

Oprah Winfrey

So you've got it, you are worthy and deserving of happiness, you need to be yourself, stay true to yourself, stand up for what you believe in, embrace all your strengths and flaws, embrace your uniqueness, be kind to yourself and others, challenge yourself, take some risks, face your fears head on, and not let others sway you or distract you from your goals and dreams. Brilliant! (phew, sounds exhausting, right?)

It might help if you have a really good idea of who you actually are, what you believe in, what your strengths and flaws are, what makes you unique and special, what risks or challenges you might like to take.

How about getting to know yourself really well?

Below are some Great Big Positive Life questions that will help you do this.

Some of them will take a lot of deep thought and reflection. Don't try and answer them all at once but do try to answer them with more than one word.

Really think about what each question could actually mean to you and try and answer them as fully as you can.

This is your chance to really express what is important to you.

You may find some of your answers surprising, inspiring and you may find some of your answers disappointing. That's ok, asking questions is a natural thing for you to do.

You definitely shouldn't feel ashamed or embarrassed about it or your answers.

Questions hold the key to unlocking a deep understanding of yourself and if we understand who we are and who we want to be we can live a happier life.

Don't judge yourself, just be honest. You can always do more of the things that make you the person you want to be, do less of the things that don't make you happy or change the things you are not happy about.

Reflection is a great way to find out about where you are right now and where you want to be in the future.

Don't over think it, there are no right or wrong answers, no one is going to be looking at what you have written (unless you want them too)

These thought provoking questions are the type of things you should ask yourself over and over again. They will help you grow, learn and challenge yourself and help you live the life you really want to lead. So grab that notebook and give it a go.

MY GREAT BIG POSITIVE LIFE
QUESTIONS

*What would I most like to change about myself ?(least
favourite qualities)* Weight, Movent, fitness

*What would I never change about myself ?(most favourite
qualities)* Shining, lovy person, fun, kind

*Is it harder to think of least favourite qualities or favourite
qualities?*

*Do I view myself in a mostly positive or mostly negative
way?*

*What other great qualities do I have (you need 3 for every
negative one you wrote)* fun, kind, Memorable

What habits would I most love to dump?
Over eating

I am most passionate about? Inspring the
people, fun, Music, world.

Other things I am passionate about?
Food, health, water

My top 5 most important values are? (What do I believe in?)
- Love -   - Respect   - Integrity
- Honesty -   Passion

The things that make me happy are?

The things that make me sad are?

Do I take things personally? (Am I overly sensitive?)

Am I guided by love or fear?

Do I worry about what other people think of me?

The things I worry about other people thinking of me are?

How would the people's opinion I value the most, actually describe me?

Do I follow the crowd or am I my own person?

What qualities do I most admire in other people?

The person that inspires me the most is?

Other people that inspire me are?

Is everyone I surround myself with adding value to my life?

The last time I did something nice for myself was?

The last time I did something nice for someone else was?

The one small act of kindness have I been shown that I will never forget is?

Do I feel good about the way I treat the most important people in my life? Am I kind?

Am I compassionate to others?

Am I a good friend?

If I could apologise to one person who would it be and what would I say?

Am I holding onto feelings that I could let go of? If so what are they?

Do I love myself as much as I expect others to love me?

What parts of my life don't reflect who I am or who I want to be?

What is it about my own company that I enjoy the most?

What kind of person do I want to be?

The last time I pushed my self out my comfort zone was?

What are the most amazing things I've achieved in the last year?

What makes me proud of myself? Do I give myself enough credit?

My dreams for the future are?

The things that excite me about my future are?

The things that most worry me about my future are?

What kind of world do I want to live in?

What could I do in my life that would help the world be a better place?

If I could go anywhere in the world where would it be and why? Maldives - Water,

What does success mean to me? (Does it include my top 5 values?)

If time and money were no object, what would I do with my life?

"Don't ever let anyone dull your sparkle, have faith and a burning desire to keep going no matter what happens.

Life many not always turn out as you had planned, but it's like a camera; focus on what's important, capture the good times, develop from the negatives and if it goes wrong... take another shot.

If it makes you happy, do it, if it doesn't, then don't, but choose what is worth fighting for and stick with your decision.If times are tough, but there is light at the end of the tunnel,

keep going.

Nothing great was ever achieved without enthusiasm and every difficulty is an opportunity in disguise.

Do what you feel in your heart to be right for you'll be criticised anyway.

The unhappiest people in the world are the ones that care most about what other people think.

Each day holds possibilities for great discoveries and hidden joy.

What appears today to be a sacrifice may prove instead to be the greatest investment you ever make.

Believe in your ability to make great things happen.

Turn your cant's into cans and your dreams into plans. Life is too short not to grab it with both hands."

LIFE LESSONS AND INSPIRATIONAL STORIES NO 3. - ED SHEERAN

A STORY OF RESILIENCE -FROM BULLIED BOY TO MUSIC ICON.

A young boy, bright ginger hair, a horrendous stutter, thick glasses and a lazy eye. Life wasn't exactly easy for the boy from Halifax. Relentlessly bullied at school he soon stopped interacting there at all and lived a life of pretty much silence during the school day.

The one thing it didn't stop him doing was singing in church. Ed always loved music, and from an early age he picked up a guitar, learnt how to play and by the age of 11 was writing his own songs. Being in his room playing his guitar was the only time he felt in control.

He knew he was made for music but with speech therapy not working he felt like he would be stuck forever.

Speaking at a New York fundraiser for the American Institute Of Stuttering he explained about his childhood stutter, and how Eminem helped him eventually get over it.

"My Uncle Jim told my dad that Eminem was

the next Bob Dylan — it's pretty similar, it's all just storytelling — so my dad bought me 'The Marshall Mathers LP' when I was nine years old, not knowing what was on it. I learned every word of it, back to front, by the time I was ten. He raps very fast and melodically and percussively, and it helped me get rid of the stutter. "

Then the hard work began. Once he had left school he moved to London.The day he arrived he emailed over 300 London music promoters asking for a gig.

50 replied and for the next 4 years he would travel around playing over 12 gigs a week, sometimes with no where to stay he was even known to sleep on the London underground Circle Line.

These gigs where not paid so it was not an easy time for the young man.

He says

" There were some bad nights where I had no money or food. There were moments I wanted to give up, I'd released four EPs. I'd played sold-out shows but I'd come out of it with no money, no place to live, and nowhere to go. "

He'd worked so hard for over four years and had nothing to show for it.

The turning point came a month later when taking his collaboration EP to yet another record company to see what they thought, for them to suggest he should just hand it out for free.

If he'd listened to their advice or just given up completely at that point he may well not be the Ed Sheeran we all know today.

Instead of sending his 5 song EP out for free he decided to put it on to iTunes to see what would happen.

Within days of him putting it up he was number 1 on the iTunes chart and from there the rest is history.

In an industry so dominated by image and looks Ed Sheeran has broken through so many barriers, going on to show that, alongside incredible talent, sheer determination, persistence, self belief, staying true to who you are, following your own path, and of course having an absolute love for what you do, you can pursue your dreams and make a success (whatever that may mean to you) of your life.

Lets reflect

The last section of this book is going to help you understand all the precious lessons you have learnt so far at a deeper level and how, by taking care of yourself (or as we are going to call it self care), you can live everyday in a clearer, focussed, more positive way.

Mind, Body and Soul is next but first lets just reflect on how far you have come.

Firstly we've looked at coming from a place of gratitude and how gratitude allows us to find happiness in what we already have. We've learnt about positive daily habits and alongside gratitude, how affirming positive beliefs can make us stronger, happier and more confident.

We've learnt about Growth Mindset, the science behind it, and how we can change the way we think about ourselves and our abilities, through the understanding that we can continue to grow the pathways and strengthen the connections in our brain with determination, effort and hard work (otherwise known as the Neuroplasticity (flexibility) of our brains).

We've looked at how setting goals can give us purpose, drive us forward and gives us space to see what it is we want to achieve and what we want out of our lives. We've learnt that persistence is key if you want to be happy and successful and that just because we can't do something now (YET) doesn't mean we won't be able to in the future. We've learnt how to fall in love with failing and how, from our biggest failures, come our biggest lessons. We've learnt that failure is part of success and that if we ever want to succeed in life we better start getting comfortable with failing on a regular basis.

We've delved again into science, this time learning about Positive Psychology and learnt that once again through practise and effort, the Nueroplasticity of our brains will allow us to change our attitudes from negative to positive. We've learnt that the more we look for (not chase) happiness, the more we can see it.

We've learnt how to make a conscious decision to welcome happiness into our lives by getting rid of the negative such as complaining, blaming, making excuses or having a negative attitude, and replacing as many negative influences as possible with positive ones.

We've learnt never to underestimate the true value in amazing friendships and how our vibe attracts our tribe. So having a positive, fun, caring, sharing personality ourselves will lead others with similar values and personalities to connect with us.

We've looked at how kindness can change us, those around us and possibly even the world. We've learnt the importance of not waiting until we get rich so we can feed the poor, but how little random acts of kindness now can make a huge difference.

We started to take the first steps on the Road to Resilience, learning and understanding that embracing our emotions, taking risks, asking for help, and staying true to who we are we can build our confidence, self belief and courage and that although our brain is powerful and very protective, we can take charge and become the boss of that brain.

Lastly we've asked The Great Big Positive Life questions and hopefully now you have a better understanding of who you are who you want to be and how you want to live your life.

PART THREE
MIND, BODY AND SOUL

Stay Curious to learn

"Take care of your body, it's the only place you have to live.

Feed your mind daily with wisdom, your body daily with good nutrition, your soul daily with joy, and every day you will thrive."

Unknown

You would think that over the years with incredible inventions such as the internet, overall better living standards, more access to money and more things to buy, people would have grown much happier and more satisfied with their lives.

In fact, the opposite seems to be true. Life has got so busy, so noisy, and so full of things, that people are losing themselves in their possessions, constantly craving more and more, and so caught up in the fast moving, ever changing world, they are actually losing sight of what makes them truly happy and are not only becoming dissatisfied with their lives, in many cases they are burning out altogether.

You want to be happy right? You want to be successful in life and you want to have lovely things? But unless you take the time to appreciate all that is around you, all the money, success, and possessions in the world just won't make you happy.

Keeping healthy in mind and body and filling your soul with all the things you love to do and that keep you fulfilled, will allow you to put all the knowledge you have gained throughout your book into practise and let you experience all the joys the world has to offer.

Being able to clear your mind, live in the moment, slow down a bit and appreciate all the great things around you is imperative if you truly want to lead a great big positive life.

SECTION 1: MINDFULNESS.
SUBSECTION A - SWITCHING OFF

"Mindfulness is simply being aware of what is happening right now without wishing it was different. Enjoying the pleasant without holding on when it changes (which it will) and being with the unpleasant without fearing it will always be this way (which it won't).

James Baraz
Master of Mindfulness

The Sound of silence.

Do you ever feel like you totally switch off? Do you ever sit in silence?

In this day and age it feels like most of the time we are switched on, plugged in, wired up. The TV or radio is always on in the background or a phone or tablet practically stuck to our face as we wonder around paying no attention to the outside world.

There is even a name for it now, "The Zombie Generation", used to describe young people who walk down the road staring at their phones with absolutely no clue what is going on around them.

There's a funny clip on YouTube of a woman walking through a shopping centre staring at her phone and she ends up going head first into a fountain of water because she didn't see it in front of her.

Ok, it's quite funny to watch, but there is a dangerous side to it too. People are beginning to walk straight onto roads, putting themselves and others at risk.

A survey of bike riders has found that it is no longer the other traffic that they feel most at risk from, it is the threat of pedestrians walking straight in front of them or even straight into them, that they worry about the most.

But there is another danger too. We are finding it harder and harder to switch off, constantly in need of entertainment in some way or another.

Studies are showing that sleep deprivation is becoming worse and more and more people are suffering with anxiety, stress, depression and other mental health related illnesses.

Although technology can't be blamed for all these problems it looks like spending lots of time attached to a device can be a contributing factor.

Our brains need a calm space to breath and grow but this is in danger by the constant digital presence in our lives.

Although a relatively new phenomenon, research is starting to come out about the actual effect that digital tech is having on our brains, and the early signs are, that although there are many great benefits to having this tech in our lives some of these benefits may be outweighed by problems caused.

Pros (positive)

Cons (negative)

Your ability to scan information rapidly and effectively can improve.

You may be unable to concentrate for any length of time, becoming bored and frustrated easily and your attention span can shorten.

Everything you want to know about anything is at your fingertips.

You may struggle to remember any of this information due to it's availability. Memory issues or lack of memory may be long term.

Your decision making and visual skills may be improved by playing fast paced computer games.

These games can also leave you struggling to control impulsive and aggressive behaviour within the game, which in turn could lead you to be impulsive and aggressive in everyday life.

Now nobody is suggesting that you should live your life with no technology or that all video games should be banned, but being aware of the pros and cons will allow you to make decisions about how much you let it take over your life.

For instance research shows that reading develops reflection, critical thinking, problem solving, and vocabulary better than visual media. So rather than looking at videos to tell you information, good old fashioned looking it up (even on the internet) and reading the information will allow you to digest it properly (if take your time and don't just scan it really quickly)

We all know that video games are fun, you can play them with your friends and they are exciting. When you win you might feel amazing, incredible even and have a rush of hormones through your body, but how do you feel when you are losing or are told you need to stop playing immediately; anxious, stressed out, emotional, angry even?

Some games are set up in a way that you have mega highs (games that go 100-1 for example) but with the mega highs can also come the mega lows.

And whilst studies have shown that video games have many positive benefits such as improved hand eye coordination, fine motor skills and strategic planning there is also now some worrying research which shows effects that can come with it that are not so positive. For instance aggression can be the negative side effect of the frustration that can be felt during a game.

The hormone (dopamine) released into the body during the highs of the game can have addictive qualities causing the player to feel anxious, stressed and upset if they can't continue to play or if they lose a game.

It seems that too much screen time can also impair brain structure and function and that the damage caused is in the frontal lobe of the brain. The frontal lobe is where most of the changes in your brain take place, especially through your teenage years. It is also frontal lobe development that largely determines your success in life from your well being, to you academic and career success to your relationships with others.

Reflection

(try to be really honest the you ask yourself...)

When playing these games how do you react if your teammates don't help you when you need them?

How do you react when you are told it is time to come off and your are in the middle of a game?

How do you react when you win? (Do you want to keep playing over and over?)

. . .

How do you react when you lose?

What do you think is happening to your brain and body during this time?

Remembering that the Neuroplasticity of your brain rewires over time with more and more exposure, do you think that this is healthy for your brain?

Remember that when you feel powerful, strong emotions of any kind, your reactions to them get imprinted into your brain and become part of who you are.

Being in control, or even being aware of how you react in these situations will help make sure you don't end up becoming a stressed, angry, over emotional person in other areas of your life.

We are looking at how we can bring more joy and happiness into your life, so it does make sense to have a good understanding of the effects technology can have on your brain. Knowing yourself, how you are feeling and how you react will allow you to make good healthy decisions about how to balance the positives with the negatives going forward.

Now get back to The Sound of Silence.

Do you find it difficult to switch off?

. . .

Do you feel that you are really noticing what goes on around you?

Do you take time to be calm, present and aware of where you are and your surroundings?

How do you feel at the prospect of being left alone, just in your own thoughts?

Is your mind full or are you "mindful"?

SECTION 1 MINDFULNESS. SUBSECTION B - WHAT IS MINDFULNESS?

"Mindfulness is simply being aware of what is happening right now without wishing it was different, enjoying the pleasant without holding on when it changes (which it will) and being with the unpleasant without fearing it will always be this way (which it won't)?

James Baraz

You may know the word "mindful" as in the context of being thoughtful. If you are being mindful of someone you are being thoughtful towards them and their feelings.

Mindfulness does mean being thoughtful, but it also means being present, aware and in the moment.

Practising mindfulness has so many benefits. It gives you the skills to be able to clear your mind and instead tune into your body. It also teaches you how to be in the moment and experience all that is around you on a conscious level.

It can help in so many ways, from recognising when you are feeling happy, to being able bring you back into the present moment when you are feeling anxious, stressed or you feel your mind wandering off into negative spaces.

Mindfulness doesn't come naturally and it takes practise but it is so worth it as it will not only allow you to experience more joy and happiness on a higher level, but it will also help you deal with challenges you face in the moment or stop you from reacting to things in a way that you may later wish you hadn't. And of course the more you practise being mindful, the stronger the connections in your brain will become, making it easier to be mindful on a daily basis.

Lets look at how mindfulness can help you recognise and imprint the feelings of joy into your memory.

So we know that we experience negative emotions both mentally, physically and deeply. There is no getting away from the sick feeling when we are anxious or the lump in our throat when we are sad.

When we experience negative emotions it's very easy to focus on them so much, that we can end up wallowing in them, allowing ourselves to become overwhelmed.

What you want to be able to do is experience the negative emotions, feel them, recognise them and then use the strategies you have learnt to deal with them so you can let them go.

Mindfulness and Mindfulness Breathing specifically, is a great way to be present with your feelings, but not give them more attention than they deserve.

Instead of wallowing in negative emotions, what we should be doing is wallowing in positive emotions such as joy, happiness and peacefulness to name a few.

Because being happy doesn't make us feel bad, we don't naturally experience the feeling on the same level as we do if we are sad for example.

You may know you are happy but do you actually take the time to really feel what happy feels like?

In order to experience more happiness you have to make a conscious decision to recognise when you are feeling happy, take a step back in the moment and take notice of how you actually feel.

Happiness, joy, and love can make you feel amazing. Just as hormones that make you feel ill are released when you face negative emotions, hormones that make you feel wonderful are released when you feel joy.

Recognising and taking notice of positive emotions will imprint them into your brain so it will automatically look for the positive rather than negative.

The brain is a powerful thing and when you are really aware of something it registers it deeply into your brain's pathways. So instead of dwelling of feelings such as sadness or anger, give it just the amount of attention it needs to be dealt with and then make a conscious decision to become mega aware each time you feel happy, joyful, relaxed, at one with yourself, chilled out, or peaceful. Taking a few moments to wallow in the positive feeling and register it deeply into your brain.

So hopefully by now you have decided that you want to be happy and welcome more joy into your life.

Now you just need the strategies to help you achieve this.

The great thing is, it's a really easy thing to do, you just have to (like with your daily affirmations and gratitudes) make it a daily habit.

The easiest way to do this, in a similar way to setting yourself goals, is to set yourself a **daily intention**. (Intention meaning you aim to feel a certain way)

Daily intentions

Setting an intention is about having your needs met.

It might be that one day you feel a bit stressed out so your intention that day would be to feel relaxed. It could be that you feel a bit down so your intention would be to feel uplifted in some way.

Setting yourself a positive daily intention will point your brain in that direction and help you become aware of all the moments that fulfil that intention throughout the day.

So once you are awake and know how you are feel you can say to yourself,

"Today I am feeling .... and my intention is to feel........................"

Then once you know what your intention is, you can write it in your planner (and don't forget your affirmations to start your day off in the right way!)

E.g. You have woken up feeling **grumpy** and **tense,** but you have decided that you want to feel joyful and relaxed. In your planner you would write...

Today my intention is to feel **joyful and relaxed**.

If you wake up feeling amazing that's brilliant (the whole point is that over time you start to feel fantastic on a regular basis), but don't forget to register your intention on these days too.

You might decide that because you feel so great you don't need to register it, but remember you are wiring your brain with powerful connections and in order to keep your brain focused on your positive feelings as a priority, you need to make sure you keep it as a priority.

So you feel great, then your intention could be to help others feel great too.

"Today my intention is to feel great and help my friends feel the same"

Lets turn some negative feelings into positive ones to help you get started.

Some other ideas for positive daily intentions could be to

feel **calm** and **content**, **relaxed** and **tranqui**l, f**ull of energy**, **clear in you mind** and **comforted**

So you have set your intention and you know how you want to feel. Next you need to understand that mindfulness is about the here and now. Being mindful is not looking to the future or being focused on the past, it is about noticing and being aware of the moments as you feel them.

You want to be able to deepen the impact of the positive times as they happen and lessen the impact of the difficult times. Hopefully, over time, you will notice that the negative experiences come less often, and when they do come, they feel smaller and easier to deal with.

After winter comes spring... just as you know the seasons will change and the weather will get better so will the difficult times in your life; they won't last forever (unless you allow them to).

Good times and bad times are the natural ebbs and flows of life. Sometimes you will feel like you are at the beach watching waves gently lapping back and forth and sometimes you will feel like you are on the biggest rollercoaster ever.

Let yourself be at one with all the ups and downs, all the great times and the bad. Don't waste your life trying to change what can't be changed, and don't try and hold on to good things that are naturally coming to an end. All you will end up with is sadness, frustration and anger, and where's the happiness in that?

Instead you are going to have the courage to deal with the difficulties and the presence to deeply experience the joy.

SECTION 1 MINDFULNESS. SUBSECTION C - MINDFULNESS BREATHING

Just Breathe

Learning how to breathe mindfully is easiest way to become present in the moment. It is something that you can practise and it has many uses.

Mindfulness Breathing allows your mind to become clear, calm and in focus.

It's a tool that you can use to;

- Enhance your experience of any given moment, reminding yourself to be aware of where you are, to enjoy it, appreciate it, breathe it all in and soak it all up.
- Help bring yourself back into the present moment, when your mind is is wandering into negative spaces or you are facing a challenge, reminding yourself to be aware of where you are, that you are ok, to breath it all out and let it all go.

- Help bring yourself in a more positive space by using some gentle affirmations while you are breathing.

Who knew that just breathing could give you so much!

Mindful Breathing isn't just any ordinary breathing, it's not just taking a few deep breaths and trying to calm down.

Mindful Breathing is being focused on the actual breath for a period of time. I's about letting thoughts enter your head (as they will) and coming back to focus on the breath whilst letting the thoughts go. It's being aware of all the sounds around you, allowing them to be in your focus but not taking your focus away from the breath.

In order to be able to use Mindful Breathing when you need it, it is best to practise it on a daily basis, even just 5 mins a day, until it becomes easy and natural for you to do.

At first you may find at the very moment you try to relax and focus on your breath, 800 different thoughts will start to enter your head. It's fine and perfectly normal for this to happen. Just go with it, let the thoughts enter, and then slowly and gently try and bring your focus back to your breath.

Each thought, let it enter and then gently focus back on your breath.

Don't let yourself get annoyed or frustrated with all the thoughts coming into focus and don't pressure yourself back to the breath, just gently and slowly try to bring the focus back.

Remember your brain is wired to think and have thoughts, so you are having to teach (rewire) to switch off, calm down and focus just on your breath.

It does take practise, so don't beat yourself up if it takes a while for this to become easier.

Use your planner to set some time for yourself just to sit and breathe, relax and focus.

How to do Mindful Breathing.

First find a place to sit, with no distractions.

It could be on a chair with your feet firmly planted on the ground, or on the floor on a cushion, with your legs crossed and your back straight. Let your hands gently sit on your lap, on your knees or you could place one hand on your chest and the other at the top of your tummy.

Close your eyes and focus on your breath, in and out, in and out. Slow your breath down, let any thoughts pass through your mind and let them go, bring your focus back to your breath slowly in and out.

Breath in through your nose and out through your mouth. Putting one hand gently on your chest and the other at the top of your tummy so you can feel your diaphragm raise up and down (try and focus your breath to that place at the top of your tummy).

Feel your body relax which each breath, let your shoulders drop and any stress or tension leave your mind and your body. Be aware of the sound of your breathing.

Just focus on your breath for a few minutes. If you like set a timer for 5 minutes so you don't need to worry that you are taking enough time (just make sure the sound of the timer is quiet and is not going to startle you when it comes on). Keep being aware of your deep breaths and how relaxed you feel.

You could gently say a few positive affirmations to yourself.

"I am safe" "I am calm" "I am loved" "I am happy" "I feel good".

After this time slowly open your eyes, still breathing deeply in and out, focus on your breathing with your eyes open for a few moments longer. Take one last another deep breath and raise your arms up to the side of your head and breath out lowering your hands back down. Give your hands a little shake away from yourself to realise any anxious energy. Then bring your breathing back to a normal pace.

Be aware of how you feel, allow yourself to feel good, allow yourself the time to be in your thoughts, allow yourself to feel calm and relaxed, until you feel ready to get up and get on with your day.

Once you have practised your mindful breathing over a period of time, and you feel confident that you can quickly bring your focus to your breath, try to incorporate it into different situations during your day.

When you feel happy, use your mindful breathing, taking a few moments and a few breaths, to indulge in that feeling of happiness.

Now when we say feeling happy, we don't just mean when you are feeling great joy. You don't need to be in the middle of a party, or having a great laugh with your friends to feel happiness.

Remember that feeling calm, relaxed, at ease, fulfilled and content are all positive emotions and you can easily dismiss these feelings because they don't come with a big high and are a bit less noticeable.

You may think your life is a bit bland and that you don't experience lots of great things. That's possibly because you just haven't taken the time to appreciate all the positive things that are around you. If you look for them you will find them.

You could be lying on your back watching the clouds, or under a starry sky, feeling relaxed.

You could be sitting on the beach and realise that you feel good and peaceful.

You could be walking your dog, and you suddenly realise you feel really free and that feeling feels great.

Or you could be sitting in your house, doing something creative like drawing, colouring or painting or reading and just feeling calm and chilled out.

Try some mindful breathing in the moments where you

just feel good, content, healthy and positive. The kind of situations that you might not previously have taken much notice of.

A little mindful breathing takes these feelings and situations into a higher place, giving you a greater sense of well being and when you start to notice and focus on moments that you would have ordinarily just let pass by, you start to realise that there is so much around you that is worth noticing and appreciating.

We can spend so much time searching or wanting things that we feel will bring us happiness, that we can easily forget that just being alive, on this incredible planet, with nature all around us, is a pretty amazing thing too.

Being present and being aware of what you have, the people in your life, the friends, you have and looking at the good things rather than just what goes wrong, can take away a lot of anxiety and stress, and bring you a sense of peace and wellbeing.

Just spending some time *"being"* rather than "doing" can allow you to appreciate all that you have and all that you are. We are called Human Beings after all...

Using Mindful Breathing in times of anxiety.

So just as we can use mindful breathing to experience greater happiness we can also use it just as effectively to interrupt negative thoughts and stop our brains wandering off into unwanted stressful anxious places.

Bringing your focus back to your breath and where you are right in that moment.

When you breathe and allow yourself to be present in moment of where you are right now, right at that second, you will realise that the moment you are in is actually fine, safe and that you are ok.

The place where you are might be much better than the place you were going in your head.

Using this technique allows you to break through those overwhelming feelings and stop them from taking over. With your breath you will start to feel calm, relaxed and the physical feelings that come with stressful thoughts will start to go.

This will allow the logical thinking part of your brain time to kick in and you will be able to deal with how you are feeling in a calmer and more logical way.

Mindful breathing is also be used to stop you you from having immediate knee-jerk reactions to things, potentially stopping you reacting in a way that you would rather you didn't.

Being able to focus quickly on your breathing, and calm your thoughts and behaviours is an amazing skill to have.

So don't miss the precious moments that go by, in search for moments that may never be and don't let moments that you would rather not be in, take over the precious moments that you already have.

" Surrender to what is.

Let go of what was.

Have faith in what will be."

Sonia Ricotti
No.1 Best Selling Author of
"Unsinkable - how to bounce
back when life knocks you down.

Mindful Breathing can help you in so many areas of your life.

For lots more on Mindful Breathing, or you if are interested in taking it to to another level with some guided meditation, just Google either mindfulness for kids, mindful breathing for kids, or guided meditation for kids and you will find hundreds of calming guided meditations that you can use on a daily basis.

Meditation is when you start by focusing on mindful breathing, you calm your body and mind and then you start to visualise how you feel and how you want to feel.

It can take practise as the brain does like to wander off into all sorts of places but with guided meditation you can listen to someone talk to you about focusing on different things that can help.

There is usually some gentle music in the background and they take you on a journey in your mind that will help relax your body, letting go of any stress within your muscles and help you relax your mind getting rid of any stressful thoughts and feelings.

Reflection

Ask yourself:

What do I feel the benefits mindfulness would be for me?

Do I think I are really aware of the world around me? Is my mind full or am I mindful?

If my mind is full, what is it full of and what would I like to let go of?

Do I ever take time to just sit and enjoy the moment I am in?

What situations do I think mindful breathing could be helpful to me in?

What do I think mindfulness does to my brain?

SECTION 2 BODY. SUBSECTION A - LETS GET PHYSICAL

Healthy Body Healthy Mind

There are so many benefits to keeping active. It helps strengthen your muscles and bones, it strengthens your lungs and your heart , it improves your energy levels, it builds your immune system and reduces the risk of diseases, such as diabetes.

But did you know, one of the biggest benefits with keeping active and fit is the effect it can have on your brain?

Exercise enhances the brain's metabolism. Studies show that active children have improved memory as a result of better brain function.

Active children have the ability to concentrate much better, even at the end of a long school day.

Exercise can literally burn off excess negative hormones and at the same time can increase the release of positive ones such as endorphins, dopamine and serotonin.

Serotonin is the chemical responsible for happiness, restful sleep, and a healthy appetite. Serotonin levels will increase if you exercise regularly, meaning more energy and clearer thinking.

Studies report that exercise decreases anxiety, reduces depression, and improves mood and outlook. In addition, your quality of sleep can also be improved.

Exercise can also improve your confidence, your self esteem and your ability to overcome challenging situations.

Wow just from keeping active and fit...

Now, we know that formal exercise is not for everyone, so before you think *"Ahhhhh" I hate exercise"*, there are many things you can do to keep fit and healthy without having to go for a ten mile run.

Getting up off your butt, switching off the TV or screen and just getting outside and just playing with friends is the best way to stay fit.

Have a game of football, tennis, join a gymnastics, swimming or dancing club. All these activities can be great fun and something to do with friends.

It doesn't need to be competitive the only thing you need to do is enjoy it as the mental and physical benefits of doing it is what counts.

If the thought of doing any kind of sport or joining a club where you have to be in front of others, fills you with dread, never fear, just get the radio on in the house and have a boogie, run up and down the stairs a few times, do some star jumps in your bedroom or just go for a walk, feel the fresh air on your face and get your heart pumping.

Exercise is about making you feel super fit and healthy which in turn will keep your body healthy and your mind positive and strong.

So go on, gimme ten...

SECTION 2 BODY. SUBSECTION B - FOOD GLORIOUS FOOD.

How Do you Eat?

In order to keep fit and healthy psychically we need to be fuelling our bodies with healthy nutritious food.

Enjoying a healthy varied diet is absolutely going to do that, but growing up having a healthy relationship with food will give you so much more.

Having a healthy relationship with food means enjoying all of it, the good, the bad and the downright outrageous.

We are brought up believing that eating healthily is good for you and eating unhealthy things like sweets and snacks is bad for you. Full stop.

But what is worse than the sugar content itself is feeling naughty for eating the unhealthy stuff in the first place. Running to the shops, buying some sweets and stuffing them into your face in the hope that no-one saw you, is not just unhealthy it's absolutely outrageous.

Not only have you filled your body with sugar so quickly that you will likely experience a crazy sugar rush and then a horrible crash and burn sore tummy and banging head, you didn't even take the time to taste, enjoy, and experience the pleasure that should be had from eating your most favourite, delicious, sticky chewy toffee or strawberry swirl.

Ok so we know that lots of sugar will do us harm and rot our teeth, but on balance the pleasure from indulging now and again will not do you any harm and in fact could do you some good as long as you take care of your teeth then it's all good!

Feeling bored and uninspired by the "healthy" food in our diets and feeling guilty for daring to go near anything with a whiff of sugar in it, is only going to lead you to have a very bad relationship with food. And there's no joy in that!

The truth is that eating mindlessly will cause you more harm than any chocolate eclair or doughnut and here's why...

When you eat mindlessly you ...

- *Can eat really quickly and easily ignore your body's signals of fullness which can lead you to overeat.*
- *Can become an emotional eater, for example when you feel bored, or sad.*
- *Can eat too fast and not actually enjoy what it is you are eating.*

- *Can eat when you are doing something else, and are distracted. Food can easily disappear without you noticing, so you have more and then feelings of guilt can take over.*
- *Can lose the enjoyment in eating altogether, and create issues with anxiety surrounding it.*
- *Before you know it you can have stuffed sweets and snacks in your face and this can result in a long-term unhealthy relationship with food.*

You might be thinking *"I'm not really to bothered about this at my age, this is something that I'll think about later"*, but now is actually the time when you start to really develop your relationship with your food, as you become independent and more in control of what you eat (school dinner money can easily be used for buying sweets instead!)

This book is all about leading a positive life so having a fantastic relationship with your food is an important part of that.

There is great joy to be had in eating, but only if we take the time to be aware of what it is we are eating, how it can make us feel and what it can do to our body.

Getting rid of the feelings of guilt surrounding the food that is supposedly bad for us is the first place to start.

Now this doesn't mean that you should spend your days filling your body with sugar and not caring about it, but if you lose the guilt and find the pleasure, you may find that you actually eat less unhealthy things, because you have taken the time to savour, taste, enjoy and experience all that you should when you're eating your favourite treat.

If you are mindful when you eat then you may even find the joy in eating your carrots and peas.

Mindful Eating

Mindful eating is just the same as being mindful in life. It's being aware, paying attention, taking the time to appreciate where you are and what you are doing.

It's not eating your tea as fast as you can so you can get back to your favourite TV programme or computer game and it's definitely not sitting at the table with your phone in front of your face whilst you eat.

It's taking notice of what you are eating, experiencing what you are eating, and it is definitely not judging what you are eating or criticising yourself for eating it.

Mindful eating allows you to...

- *Slow down, and listen to your body for signals of when you are full, thus stopping you from over eating (it takes 20 mins for your stomach to tell your head you are full)*
- *Eat when you are hungry and your body tells you to eat, not just because you are bored or want to feel better. i.e it allows you to listen to your body's needs and wants.*

- *Enjoy your favourite treats now and again, experiencing the pleasure and none of the guilt.*
- *Eat food not stories. i.e. that eating healthy food is boring, or eating unhealthy food is bad.*
- *Appreciate where your food has come from, and who has taken the time to provide you with it.*
- *Give yourself a chance to try new foods, and really find out what you enjoy and what you don't.*
- *Have a lifelong love of good food, an interest in food, which in itself can bring you a life full of exciting flavours, taste sensations, visual delights, and new experiences.*

It's not a surprise that we are in a place where so many of us eat mindlessly. Everything is so fast and busy nowadays and it does feel like there's not enough time. Being constantly plugged in, doesn't help. Eating when distracted is a sure fire way for you to eat way more than you would or that your body needs because your food has disappeared in front of your eyes without you even noticing.

So how do we go about eating mindfully?

It's pretty easy, just start by being aware of what is going into your mouth.

Take notice: of what it smells like, what it tastes like, what it makes you feel like, and what it does to your body (now remember no feeling guilty)

Switch off: put down the book, the phone, the tablet and step away from the TV.

Mindful Snacking

The next time you are having a snack e.g a packet of crisps and you are in front of a book or screen, try reading a few pages or watching a little bit, pause what you are doing and enjoy a few mouthfuls of your snack, notice it, taste it and enjoy it, then go back to what you are doing, pause again and have a little bit more.

Be aware of how much you have eaten over a period of time. You may be surprised that you have eaten less than you would normally have done.

You may find you feel fuller than you normally would have. You may find that one snack is enough where previously you would have been looking for something else.

The next time you have a chocolate bar, try cutting it in half, and do the same; each bite you take, make sure you are not distracted, pause what you are doing and enjoy how amazing that chocolate really is. Or better still get your self a drink, sit quietly on your own and enjoy that bit of chocolate in all its glory.

Recognise how you feel afterwards, it is so worth the calories if you really enjoyed it.

So no more mindlessly stuffing packets of crisps and sweets into your mouth for no reason, without even noticing you have had them, no enjoyment, no fun, no taste sensation, no point.

Treats and snacks should be enjoyed to their fullest or not had at all.

Try eating an apple mindfully, knowing that it is a healthy option but is also a really tasty, sweet, crunchy, enjoyable snack. Take your time again with no distractions, really indulge in it's sweetness and juiciness.

How amazing does this apple seem now?

Knowing that something is good for you doesn't necessarily mean that it is boring. Some of the most amazing food in the world can also be some of the healthiest for you.

Mindful Meal Times

When you are called for tea and your usual response would be to grudgingly come to the table, or to complain that you can't have it in front of the TV, try using it as an opportunity for you to be mindful. Taking the time to switch off a bit, taking a break from being busy to relax a bit, slow down and actually appreciate it it may be a time for something really special.

Time to spend and talk to the people you live with, time for them to find out about your day, take an interest in what you are doing, what you have to say and your opinion.

A mindful mealtime can be a time to connect with others, share good food and for you to be aware of all the good things you have in your life.

A roof over your head, a delicious meal to eat and people who care about you.

Don't view mealtimes as annoyance that it has taken you away from what you are doing, but an opportunity to chill out, reflect, chat, and to enjoy your food in a mindful way.

Maybe the next mealtime, you can share what you have learnt about mindful eating.

How to enjoy a mindful mealtime.

Instead of waiting to be called to the table, offer to help set the table, bring the food or even better help cook the meal. Get involved and use this time to chat and enjoy each other's company. If you don't have a table that's fine, every family is different, but you can still help get things ready.

When you are ready to eat, sit down and take a few mindful breaths. Really appreciate what it is you are about to eat, smell the smells, enjoy what it looks like and take a moment (before you decide there is something on the plate that you don't like) to value all whats on the plate that you will really enjoy.

It's amazing how when we engage with our veggies for instance how good they can actually taste.

Learning about where your food came from can also give you an appreciation of it that you may not previously have had, and can also add some conversation to the table. We have lost interest in our food's journey due to how easily it is readily available and as such we have lost the connection to our food.

What we eat is as important as the sun and sky, and taking an interest may bring a positive attitude to all the different kinds of food that our world has to offer.

Eat slowly, savouring every mouthful and appreciating what it is giving you, from the pleasure of it's taste, to the nutrients and fuel it is giving your body.

Again try not to multitask while having a mindful meal. You may have been told it's bad manners to talk with your mouth full but actually if you're talking whilst eating then you can't be fully aware of what is in your mouth.

So have a mouthful, have a chat, have another mouthful and so on, encouraging everyone at the table to take their time, Enjoying each other's company and enjoying your food will leave you feeling full, content, cared for and connected.

Hopefully you'll never look at food in the same way again.

SECTION 2 BODY. SUBSECTION C - SLEEP

So you got to bed late, you didn't get much sleep and you feel pretty groggy this morning, you go to school, have a bit of trouble concentrating, and couldn't really be bothered. You might be a bit cranky and have a bad attitude but it's not the end of the world right?

Well, did you know that research has found that sleep is absolutely essential to your overall good health? When you get the sleep you need, you may have a lower risk of becoming overweight and developing diseases such as diabetes when you are older, as well as fewer learning problems and attention issues.

Now we don't want to bore you to sleep on this one so let's just do a quick overview of why sleep is essential and how you can get a better night's sleep.

If you think of your brain and your body as a battery, by the end of the day you will obviously need to recharge it. Sleep is the power source, but do you know all the things that actually happen to you when you are asleep and why getting enough sleep per night it is as important to your health as keeping fit and eating well?

Your body needs sleep to:

Help you grow, strengthen your immune system, and help you to fight off infections.

Repair cells and help you fix existing injuries and reduce further injury risk.

Your brain needs sleep to:

Build your brain cells and help you remember what your learnt during the day

Help boost learning (you actually learn in your sleep).

Help you pay attention and concentrate,solve problems and think of new ideas.

Help you be a nice person, a better friend.

Did you know that the 10 key things you need to be happy also happen to spell GREAT DREAM (and we've only got M to go)

So how much sleep do we need and how do we get a good sleep?

How much sleep you need mainly depends on your age. Young people from the age of 9 to about 14 need roughly between 10 and 12 hrs sleep per night in order for them to function really well on a daily basis.

Everyone is individual so you may need a little less or a little more.

Having a good bedtime routine, getting to bed at roughly the same time and waking up at the same time, can help you get a better, more settled night's sleep as your internal body clock (connections in your brain) likes the repetition.

In order to get the best sleep you need to be able to switch off your brain.

In particular, watching TV, being on a games console, phone or tablet close to bedtime has been associated with not wanting to go to bed, difficulty falling asleep, anxiety around sleep and sleeping fewer hours.

The blue light associated with devices can also give you the impression it is still day time so switch them off at least an hour before bed and do something else that will allow your brain to clam down and switch off.

Bedtime tips

Switch off all other devices at least an hour before bed.

Have a glass of milk and a healthy snack low in sugar (toast or cracker)

Write down your gratitudes.

Read a book/Kindle. (Kindles don't produce the blue light as other devices do, so you are all good)

Make sure your too is not too hot. Your body temp drops

during sleep so get your body ready so you drift off comfortably.

When you turn off the light make sure your room is dark.

Do some mindful breathing or listen to a guided meditation.

Get some exercise during the day as it improves the length and quality of your sleep at night.

SECTION 3 SOUL.

Let your soul sing and your heart be full of joy

When we talk about your soul we are talking about your very being.

Some people describe the soul as an energy that is part of you, not physical as such, but a deep part of you that makes you who you are.

The word heart is often used in the same way or put together with soul.

"That person is a jolly soul" meaning that they have a happy disposition (or happy nature).

"That person has a kind heart" meaning they are kind and compassionate to others.

So your soul is your internal character, your personality, it's what makes you think in a certain way, act in a certain way and what makes you believe in certain things.

If you did some "soul searching" it would involve deep thinking as to why you feel things in a certain way, or your motives as to why you act in a certain way, or make certain choices.

For the purposes of this book we are looking at how you can lead a positive life by filling your heart and soul with joy, happiness and meaning.

What makes your soul sing, makes your heart happy, what do you really enjoy that makes you feel good, what makes you feel good about yourself, and what will give your life meaning and purpose(what fulfils you)?

What fills your heart with joy?

There are so many things that we can talk about that can fill your heart with joy, things like music, singing, dancing, reading, writing, painting, being creative, playing sport, playing a musical instrument, learning new things, walking, nature, animals, spending time with friends, spending time with loved one are just a few, the list could go on and on.

Music

Finding joy in music can give you a life time of happiness. There will always be songs that you will love or that will mean something special to you. Certain music can make you feel really happy or if you feel sad there is always a song or piece of music that can reflect that too.

Music has the capacity to make you feel things deeply and that's what we want to fill your soul with. Singing or dancing along to music when you feel down can help you feel better and just going crazy and letting yourself get lost in the music can make you feel free and exhilarated (very very happy).

Music can also be linked to special memories, so making a collection of your favourite songs is a great way to collect memories (and in the long run collecting happy memories will make you feel much better than just collecting things).

Make a music list as you come across songs that are important to you, or that you just love and make you feel happy.

Reading

Reading is one of the most incredible ways to fill your soul. It calms your brain, it slows you down, it allows you to be peaceful, quiet and take some time for yourself. But the best bit about reading is that you get to open your mind and go on amazing adventures that can stay with you for a lifetime.

You can go to places you never thought existed, you can use your own imagination, rather than, like watching TV, where it's all imagined for you. Reading is a deeply personal experience and although you could tell someone else the storyline, only you know what the story looked like and felt like to you.

Reading can be funny, sad, exciting, scary, and magical, it can make you think, it can challenge you and inspire you. Reading gives you words, knowledge and understanding that you didn't have before, it can make you smarter and more interesting.

Some books will have a huge impact on you, some not so much, but after each book you will be different in some way with a different story to tell.

Some books you will want to read over and over again, so making a collection of your favourite books going forward can help you get all your favourite reads in one place.

Don't forget to write how you felt after you finished, so if you fancy feeling like that again you will know which one to go back to first.

Being Outside

From feeling the fresh air on your face, hearing the birds sing, looking for as many animals as you can find, enjoying the sunshine or rain (if you like getting wet), being with nature can make you feel a sense of peace and can also be lots of fun.

Nowadays we spend so much time indoors in front of the TV, or on games consoles, that we can forget that the same feelings that you get from watching TV or playing video games can be felt in the good old outdoors and it's so much better for our bodies and our brains.

There's nothing like a good walk when you are feeling stressed out, upset or cross about something, or even just plain bored. Getting up and outside, being surrounded by nature and filling your lungs with fresh air, allows you to clear your mind, calm your thoughts and feelings, appreciate what you already have in the world and allows you to bring yourself into the present and just take some time for you.

When you feel tired it may just be that you need to get outdoors for a bit of a vitality boost, increasing your energy levels and also releasing the happiness hormone (serotonin).

Getting outdoors is not just good for your mind, it's great for your body too. Fresh air is known to increase the oxygen in your body which strengthens your immune system.

We have obviously talked about how being stuck behind a console for hours on end is not doing your brain a lot of good, so if one of the reasons you love playing computer games is because you can play with your friends, how about meeting them and playing outside for a bit instead.

Be it hours on a computer or hours studying really hard, taking a break and recharging the batteries outside will make you feel more energised, more alert and happier.

Getting Creative

From being able to lose yourself in a painting for hours and hours to becoming someone else at your drama group, being creative has long been thought of as one of the most fundamental requirements to a happy and fulfilled life.

Enjoying films at the cinema, plays at the theatre, going to the museum or art galleries are fantastic ways to expand your mind and fill your soul with joy.

As children being creative can be an everyday experience. Using your imagination and expressing yourself through creativity is fun, freeing and teaches you many skills, but as you grow into adulthood you can very easily lose this really important part of your life.

Higher education especially can leave you in a place where you may feel that creative subjects don't hold the same regard as academic subjects and that the skills learnt through creative subjects aren't as valuable as the skills learnt within Maths and Science for example.

The truth is that creative industries are the fastest growing industries today, offering a huge amount of jobs and paying a huge amount towards global economies'.

From Artists, Musicians, Writers and Actors, Fashion Designers, Architects and Entrepreneurs (people who create and start their own businesses from scratch), to jobs in Software and Digital Media Design, Web Design, Visual Arts, Photography, Advertising, Marketing, Public Relations, Events Management, Art Direction, Theatre Direction, Set Design, Interior Design, Floristry, Jewellery Design, Animation, Illustration, Special Effects, Screen Writing, Editing, Choreography, Composing, and that's only some of the jobs that have been invented.

The word is changing so quickly and so is the job market and the chances are by the time you get to working age, the job that you may be doing in the future might not even exist at the moment. How exciting is that!!!!

Sometimes the pressure to do well academically can quash your creative spirit.

Remember

"You are so much more than just a spelling test"

Donna Pentony
Very special Teacher

There is no doubt that education and having a love of learning will help you achieve amazing things but education and learning don't necessarily mean having to be academic.

Never let yourself feel inferior because you enjoy creative subjects more than academic subjects. The world needs creative minds and makers for it to evolve and grow.

Steve Jobs the creator of Apple, talks about his success at creating the Mac computer:

"Part of what made the Macintosh great was that the people working on it were musicians and poets and artists and zoologists and historians who also happened to be the best computer scientists in the world..."

Incredible skills can be learnt from being creative. You have to make your own decisions, you need to be willing to put yourself out there, and also be able to accept criticism.

You will have to be dedicated and put in many hours of

work and practise in order to achieve great results. Being creative requires you to really stretch yourself, your mind and imagination.

Taking a creative path doesn't necessarily mean you're taking a soft path or easy path. Often it means the absolute opposite.

Having creativity in your life can give you a sense of enormous wellbeing, a sense of peace, a sense of fulfilment and accomplishment. There is joy, fun and freedom in being creative, it can also give you balance in your life.

Never lose that inner artist, singer, dancer, writer, actor or designer; you never know where it may take you to.

Who knows you could become the next Ben Towers: Entrepreneur (Google him), JK Rowling: Writer, Mark Zuckerberg: Creator of Facebook, Kelly Hoppen: Interior Designer, or Ed Sheeran: Musician

Why not create your own collections of the things that you enjoy doing the most.

A collection of your favourite creative hobbies, a collection of fantastic memories you have had with family or friends, a collection of things you have found when you were out on a nature walk, a collection of things you found at the beach. It doesn't matter what it is, just make it personal to you.

"True happiness if found in collecting moments not things"

FINAL WORDS

Let's end with some inspiration from who I think are two of the most inspirational women in the world today. These two gorgeous girls are the Co-Founders of Female Success Network.

A special environment that they have created, where they coach and mentor other women to succeed in life and in business.

"Courage is not the absence of fear"

Abigail Horne
Co-Founder of FSN
No. 1 Best Selling Author
Entrepreneur, Publisher and Business Coach
and an all round incredible human being.

What Abi is saying is that being courageous doesn't mean that you aren't scared. Being courageous means that you are scared, but you are willing to do it anyway because it is worth doing and means so much to you.

So go out and be courageous with your dreams and goals, never let anyone try and undermine them, change them or distract you from achieving them. Be creative with your choices, find things that you truly love, things that inspire and fulfil you. And don't stop till you achieve what you set out to achieve. The path may change, embrace it, reorganise it but never give up on it.

"The power is within you to change your belief system from limiting to empowering in one decision"

Sarah Stone
Co-Founder of FSN
No. 1 Best Selling Author
Entrepreneur, Strength and Business Coach
and another all round incredible human being

What Sarah is saying is if you don't believe you are capable of achieving something, you never will, BUT you do have the power within you to decide whether you live a life of self-doubt, or a life of self belief.

It's one decision, your decision, to either limit yourself or empower yourself.

I know what I would love you to do...

Conclusion for parents.

I really hope that through reading this book you will have gained an insight into the world of Positive Psychology, Growth Mindset and Mindfulness and are able to see that by having this information from a young age negative behaviours, patterns and feelings can be prevented from manifesting in the first place.

Obviously as I have included exactly what is covered in the journal it has meant that the activities and strategies throughout are not age appropriate for you as parents but, if you are wanting to continue your own personal self care journey and I encourage you to do so, I can highly recommend Niyc Pidgeon's book Now Is Your Chance - A 30 Day Guide To Living Your Happiest Life using Positive Psychology and also You Can Heal Your Life by the award winning writer Louise Hay.

Good Luck on leading a Great Big Positive Life.

With Lots of Love

Lorna xxx

ACKNOWLEDGMENTS

Dr. Carol S Dweck PHD

I would like to acknowledge the great and powerful work of Dr Carol S. Dweck. Professor of Psychology at Stanford University. Dr Dweck is widely regarded as one of the worlds leading researchers in the fields of personality, social psychology and developmental psychology. Her book "Mindset: Changing the way you think to fulfil your potential" is the book that inspired me to start my mission to help as many children as possible to develop a better understanding of who they are, who they want to be and how they can fulfil their full potential.

Catriona Gill MA(HONS) PSYCH, PGDE, DIPC.

I would also like to acknowledge the advice and support I have received from Catriona during the writing of the journal. Having professional guidance has been invaluable to the process and I appreciate all she has done to help me along the way.

ABOUT THE AUTHOR

LORNA PARK

Lorna Park is a mum on a mission. Creator and co-founder of My Great Big Positive Life, she is passionate about helping children develop a deeper understanding of their own Mind, Body and Souls using the principles of Growth Mindset, Positive Psychology and Mindfulness.

Worried about the increasingly stressful, noisy world our children are living in, whether it be from the endless succession of testing them from a very early age, the rise of social media and the constant comparison that comes with it, or the never-ending need to be entertained, Lorna feels that sadly, not only are the days of having a carefree childhood gone, but that children are not able to switch off in order to create a clear and calm space in which to grow.

Through her own personal study into the recent developments of Neuroscience, and inspired by the work of Positive Psychologists and Authors such as Dr. Carol Dweck, Niyc Pidgeon, and Arianna Huffington, she truly believes that once we understand how our brains work and develop, we are able unlock the key to our own future happiness and success.

Inspired by the changes in her son Charlie (11), and seeing first hand the impact working on Growth Mindset, Positive Psychology and Mindfulness has had on his own self belief, resilience, persistence, stress levels and over all health, but disappointed in the resources available to him, she has created the "My Great Big Positive Life Journal", for children, so they can empower themselves with the techniques and knowledge that will allow them grow into strong, powerful, unique individuals, comfortable with who they are and able to live their own great big positive life.

The first of it's kind in the UK, My Great Big Positive Life Journal "Superstar" Edition (for ages 9+) guides it's owner through each of the principles using different methods such as reading, creative writing, activities and exercises. Encouraging personal engagement, the journal is a place to develop positive daily habits, a place for self reflection, a place to set individual goals and measure outcomes, and offers space such dream space and genius space to encourage imagination.

Covering a wide range of topics such as "Making Friends With Failure" "How to Rewire Your Brain" "Just Breathe" "Mindfulness Matters" "Random Acts of Kindness" "Dream Big" "Attitudes of Gratitude" "Choose Happy" " The Power of Yet" "You Ain't Nothing But A Goal Digger" "Stay True To Who You Are" and many more, the emphasises is on the child to develop their own individual journal of joy, at their own pace and create something special and unique to them.

Lorna is now devoted to spreading the My Great Big Positive Life messege far and wide and alongside her journal for tweens and teens is busy expanding her business to include self care workshops, essential oils for children and young adults and of course bringing to life the much awaited journal for ages 5+.

CONTACT:

Email: mygreatbigpositivelife@gmail.com

Website: mygreatbigpositivelife.co.uk

facebook.com/mygreatbigpositivelife

instagram.com/mygreatbigpositivelife

16 — Sixteen

Someone You Loved

Lewis Capaldi

40823912R00123

Printed in Poland
by Amazon Fulfillment
Poland Sp. z o.o., Wrocław